Living In The
Last Days

Living in the Last Days

An in Depth Look at Bible Prophecy, Current Events, and How They Relate to You

CAROL McCORMICK

International Award-winning Author

Celestial Press
New York

Living in the Last Days: An in Depth Look at Bible Prophecy, Current Events, and How They Relate to You

carolmccormick.com

Paperback: 978-0-9675368-6-6

Hardcover: 978-0-9675368-7-3

Truth without love is like surgery without anesthesia.
Love without Truth is like anesthesia without surgery.

In other words...

Truth without love may hurt a person.
Love without Truth will ruin a person.

Jesus Christ is both Love and Truth.
He is also the Living Word of God.

Truth must be linked to the authority of the scriptures.
This book is based on that authority.

Those rich in wisdom and ruled by Truth
are not controlled by their emotions.

CONTENTS

The Bible is the only book that tells humans how they can live forever. As astounding as this fact may be, it is just as astounding that many people choose not to receive it.

Peter asked Jesus, *"Lord, to whom shall we go? You have the words of eternal life"* (John 6:68).

My Conversion

Ever since I became a Christian, Bible prophecy has fascinated me. It is what originally sparked my search for the Truth about God, life, the end times, and my eternal destination.

Prior to my conversion, I had no interest in spiritual things and very little knowledge of God's Word. I knew a few Bible stories and rote prayers from the occasional times I attended religious instruction or church while growing up, but the lessons and messages bored me, so I often skipped classes and mass to go hang out with friends instead.

Then, a few months before I turned 21, my world began to shift. I had just come out of an abusive relationship and was fumbling in the dark while trying to find my way in life. My search was going nowhere, until one day while visiting my aunt, a glimmer of light shined from a shelf in the form of a book about survival. Thinking it was about basic life skills or camping in the wilderness, I happily took it home.

The book was *not* about life skills or camping in the wilderness. It was about strange sounding events that I'd never heard of before, like people being caught up in the clouds to meet Jesus in the air, and being changed from mortal to immortal in the twinkling of an eye.

Humph! This is ridiculous! I thought. *Sounds like something out of a sci-fi movie.*

The book also said things like judgment and disasters would befall those on earth, and then seven years later Jesus Christ would return to set up his Kingdom.

Never heard that before either.

This new futuristic info was absolutely foreign to me, but I kept reading anyway. And as I did, I noticed smaller words and numbers below these statements, and somehow I knew they were Bible verses. I immediately dug out an old Bible (that I had never read), looked up the verses and there they were! Those strange quotes were really in the Bible! Well, I got scared. I knew that I would be left behind when this momentous event occurred, because I had been living a life of rebellion and hell.

It was then that I began searching for God, and six months later after many dead ends, my quest led to a meeting where the speaker gave her testimony. As she spoke, I thought she was talking directly to me when she described her wild past and wayward ways. I thought she could see into my heart when she mentioned her list of sins, yet there she stood saying that she was going to heaven someday.

Well that's impossible! I thought. *Especially after all she'd done. No one can know that until after they die anyway.*

Then she quoted more verses that were unfamiliar to me: *"All we like sheep have gone astray; We have turned, every one, to his own way; And the Lord has laid on Him the iniquity of us all"* (Isaiah 53:6).

She went on to say, *"For all have sinned and fall short of the glory of God,"* and *"For the wages of sin is death, but the gift of God is eternal life in Christ Jesus our Lord"* (Romans 3:23; 6:23).

Every time she quoted a verse my heart fluttered like a butterfly had flown into my chest. It was like nothing I'd ever felt before.

When the luncheon ended, I stayed behind to confront this woman who made such a bold proclamation, because I too, wanted forgiveness and the assurance that I would be in heaven someday. I told the speaker that I wanted to become a Christian, but I couldn't stop sinning.

She led me to a nearby couch where we sat down, and then she explained that God saves us by His grace when we repent and receive Jesus Christ as our Savior.

This couldn't be all there was to it, because I knew *who* Jesus was and believed that he was a real person, and yet my life was filled with sin, guilt and defeat. This answer seemed too simple, so I challenged her again by saying this was impossible for me, because of the awful things I had done. (I had surmised that since she didn't know what my life was really like, that her message didn't apply to me. She didn't know about the times I had run away from home and lived on the streets for weeks. She didn't know about the run-ins with the police, or the risky things I had done, or that my habitual drinking had escalated dramatically since I was fourteen years old.)

Yet, this wonderful woman patiently continued by quoting a verse that said, *"For by grace you have been saved through faith, and that not of yourselves; it is the gift of God, not of works, lest anyone should boast"* (Ephesians 2:8-9).

I challenged her again, and asked, "Where is that in the Bible?"

And she'd patiently show me. We went around like this a few more times, because I could not believe that God loved me and that His gift of salvation was free.

Each time I protested and asked her for proof, she'd flip through her Bible, and I'd lean over to read the words for myself. *"If you confess with your mouth the Lord Jesus and believe in your heart that God has raised Him from the dead, you will be saved. For with the heart one believes unto righteousness, and with the mouth confession is made unto salvation. Whoever calls on the name of the Lord shall be saved"* (Romans 10:9-10, 13).

I was so ignorant of the gospel that I thought I had to be good first before receiving Christ, but this woman said, "Repentance *is* in order, but when you receive Jesus as Savior, *He* gives you new desires and the power to do His will." *For it is God who works in you both to will and to do for His good pleasure* (Philippians 2:13).

This made sense to me, because I had tried to quit my sins, addictions, and dysfunctional behaviors on my own and failed miserably every time. But if He was the One giving me new desires, it must also be up to Him to provide the power to overcome.

The speaker showed me another promise that said, *"Not by works of righteousness which we have done, but according to his mercy He saved us"* (Titus 3:5).

This verse was the clincher. I finally understood that it wasn't what I had done or not done, but what Jesus did on the cross that saved me. It was only by His mercy and grace that I could be forgiven and given eternal life.

After this last time of seeing the Truth in black and white, I was ready to pray with her. I bowed my head, and in my mind, I thought: *I'm tired of going my own way and making a mess of my life. I don't care what friends or possessions I lose, I want You* (God)*, forgiveness, and heaven.*

With these thoughts, I had unwittingly repented of my sins and unconditionally surrendered my life to Christ. I had mentally stepped over the line and pushed all my chips in the pot. I was all in, willing to lose everything, to gain what Jesus offered instead.

The woman led me in a prayer that changed my life, as I bowed my head and asked Jesus to forgive me, and to come into my heart and save me. And when I did, something dramatic happened. A huge burden lifted from my shoulders and something literally swept through me. I instantly felt clean inside and God moved in.

This wasn't something I could have conjured up on my own, because I didn't know what to conjure up. Before this time, I knew nothing of the Holy Spirit or God's forgiveness or peace. I had no preconceived idea of what to envision or expect, but something had changed inside of me. I instantly knew that I was forgiven and free. Free of guilt and shame and given a second chance. My immediate thought was, *No one can point a finger at me and whisper anymore.*

I had been born-again, without even knowing what the term meant or that there even was such a thing.

Because of my lack of biblical knowledge, I had no preconceived ideas about the Scriptures or prophecy. This worked in my favor as I began to devour the Word and read it with unbiased eyes. And within two years, I had read most of the New Testament a dozen times, along with much of the Old Testament.

God's Word became the new foundation my life was built upon. The grid and filter that sifted Truth from error, so that choices were made with this new eternal perspective in view. And since the day of my salvation, in good times and bad, in victories and defeats, I have continued to read the Bible and have watched prophecies unfold ever since.

My walk with the Lord has not been perfect. I have swayed, strayed, stumbled, and fallen *many times* (and still do). It happens to any runner in a race. But during these setbacks, I was still headed in the right direction while God's love patiently lifted me every time. His Word and the still small voice of the Holy Spirit guided me like a compass back to the straight path. His grace was sufficient. His strength was enough. My lesson was learned, and I moved forward.

Why I Wrote this Book

When writing and promoting a book, marketers advise authors to know their target audience in order to reach them. As I pondered this suggestion, I realized that this book is for all people, because someday, it will affect everyone, everywhere, in one way or another.

There are many people who have never heard of Christ's forgiveness and gift of eternal life, or what the Bible says about *Living in the Last Days*, so I wrote this book for the lost, to give insight and clarity to these events, so they will know how to prepare for them. Prophecy is what initially piqued my curiosity about God and my eventual hunger for the Bread of Life, Jesus. I pray that it will create a desire for you and others to seek Him too.

I also wrote this book for Christians who have drifted away from sound Biblical doctrine and the fundamentals of the faith, to encourage them to study the Word and get back on track, so they too will be ready for Christ's return.

This book is also for those who believe in their own version of truth or God. I say, *their own version*, because many people who hold these *truths* have never really read the Bible, to learn what the Word really says about God, or to discover what His will is for them.

This book is also for those who simply want a better understanding of prophecy, to help them unpack the book of Revelation, so they can be aware and prepare for future events too. Ultimately, this book is for everyone who thirsts for the Truth, which is found in Jesus Christ (John 8:32).

This is by no means an exhaustive study, since it is impossible for even the most learned scholars of eschatology (the study of end times) to mine the depths of God's Word. But I will explain to the best of my ability and research, a tentative timeline of prophetic events and how they coincide with current events.

I also encourage you to **do your own research**. Temporarily put aside what preachers have told you, what others have told you, or what you've read on the Internet. Instead, look up the scriptures for yourself, to see the words in black and white (or red). Examine the evidence presented here and then make your own decisions. I have kept all Bible references close to each quote, so you can do your own fact-check by comparing and seeing for yourself that what I have written is not my opinion, but what the Bible clearly states.

The following are just a few examples of erroneous and unscriptural teachings that have been passed down through the ages.

- Eve did not eat an apple in the Garden of Eden. The name of the fruit is never mentioned.

- Jesus was not born in a barn-like stable, but rather a rock-like cave.

- No one knows the actual date of Christ's birth, but it was more likely in September.

- There is no mention of *three* kings visiting the infant Jesus, but there were at least two (possibly more) wise men who visited Jesus a year or two later when he would have been a toddler.

There are more examples, but these are enough to make the point. Believing these particular fallacies will not make a difference in a person's eternal destination, but other misconceptions can, if the fraud concerns the gospel or doctrinal issues.

It is easy to accept tradition or take what people say as truth, when in reality, tradition and people are not always accurate. This is why it is so important to read and study the Word for ourselves. Bible literacy is of utmost importance in discerning the Truth from error.

Since the best commentary on the Bible is the Bible, most of the prophecies mentioned in Revelation are supported by other prophecies in the Old and New Testaments. These writings were penned by many different authors who lived centuries and miles apart from each other. The cohesiveness of their writings points to One author, God, as the Holy Spirit spoke through them when they wrote.

This miraculous fact is why the Bible is my primary source of research and reference when interpreting Revelation and other prophecies. In the decades of my wondering and learning about prophecy, I have had many unanswered questions, but since I began this book almost three years ago, the still small voice of the Holy Spirit has shown me key pieces to the puzzle. He has helped me unravel and understand many prophetic scriptures as I sought them out, and then compared, dissected and put them back together again.

I do not know all the answers or how prophecy will ultimately unfold, but what I have written in this book makes the most sense to me, when compared to other views I have heard or read in the past.

The information in this book has not only been gathered first and foremost from the Bible, but also from news sources and historical evidence. All of the quotes and websites I reference are readily accessible through a simple Internet search that can be found online at credible sites. I have provided links to many of them at the end of this book.

You may not agree with some of the things that I've written in this book, and that's okay. The dispute is not with me, but with the Word of God. Therefore, I encourage you to question what you've been taught or heard, and then ask yourself if what you have learned is based on religious tradition or Scripture. The easiest way to know the Truth is to look up the verses cited in this book or read the Bible for yourself.

Many things referenced here concerning Jesus may surprise some people. The meek Jesus we see in art, movies, or select scriptures is only one side of Christ. Yes, He is Love incarnate, gentle and kind, but He is also Judge and King, who will tread the grapes of wrath himself and rule His kingdom with an iron rod (Revelation 19:15).

We do not hear many sermons about this side of Christ. Some preachers and people find the teachings of Jesus controversial. Some don't like or agree with the cringeworthy parts in the Word, so they stop short of the difficult passages, or completely omit them from their sermons.

My question then is, *Did Jesus not mean those things that He said? Was he joking when he preached the parts that make us quake?* Of course not! Not when it concerns the eternal state and destiny of a soul. Not when the main purpose of His coming to earth was to seek and to save those who are lost (Luke 19:10).

If we believe the Bible is true and that Jesus did everything with intention, then we must ask ourselves why He preached these controversial things, and then adjust our response to His teachings.

Taking a false preacher at his word can be lethal in the end, which is why it is important, to not only read the Bible, but to also *know* the Bible. Teaching a distorted version of God's Word, to those who don't know any better, is like serving arsenic-laced cake to guests at a party who happily eat it up, while never questioning what they swallow. It may taste fine at the time, but this lack of knowledge will kill them in the end.

We must learn to discern Truth from error by studying the Bible for ourselves. Biblical knowledge lays out all the ingredients, so we know what we are consuming.

There is also a special blessing for those who read Revelation: *Blessed is he who reads and those who hear the words of this prophecy, and keep those things which are written in it; for the time is near* (Revelation 1:3).

It seems that by keeping this future view in the forefront of our minds, it has a way of changing how we live our lives. This expectancy puts our priorities in order and

21

aligns our will with God's will, which makes it easier to walk the straight path that leads to life. Keeping this eternal perspective in view also helps us deal with hardships on earth, because we know and believe that life on earth is temporary, and a far greater glory awaits us in heaven.

One other aside I must mention is that there is some repetition in this book. Many scriptures and points are repeated, not only to support complementary passages and events, but also to clarify text for readers who choose to only read specific chapters that interest them. It is also because certain passages are so rich in information, that part of the verse is used to support one topic, and another part of the verse is used to support a different topic.

My ultimate prayer in writing this book is that souls will be saved and lives will be changed. The greatest journey a person will ever take is following Christ with their whole heart.

What if?

What if you were having coffee with your friends and they suddenly vanished? Or, what if you were the one who disappeared and you were safe in heaven, but your friends, coworkers, or adult family members were left behind to live through a time of terrible disasters and judgment? Even worse, what if they managed to survive that time, but didn't make it to heaven in the end?

What if the rapture isn't at the beginning of the Tribulation, but is at the end instead? Would your faith be strong enough for you to stand for Christ, even if it costs you your life? Are you concerned enough about family and friends, who do not know the Lord, that you are willing to share your faith with them?

What if someone you loved were to buckle under during the future tyrannical rule and take the Mark of the Beast for the sake of food and safety? Would you wish that you had talked to them and told them how to prepare for this coming time?

These are questions we must ask ourselves, because we need to know our options and where each decision will lead us and others. Doing nothing is doing something by default. The answer is always "no" by default, until we choose to say "yes" to Biblical Truths.

Prophetic events are lining up daily that will lead to their fulfillment. We only need to open our eyes to see that this is true. The rapture will take place sometime in the near future, but since we don't know when it will be, we should prepare now.

Ruth Graham, wife of evangelist Billy Graham, made a profound statement that sums up all rapture stances when she said, *"I would rather prepare myself to go through the tribulation and be happily surprised by an unexpected rapture, than expect to be raptured only to find myself going through the tribulation. Perhaps not a very scholarly way of approaching the problem, but true nonetheless."*

Great advice, not only for the rapture, but also for life itself, since no one knows when their earthly clock will stop.

Corrie Ten Boom was arrested by the Germans and sent to a concentration camp for the crime of hiding Jews during the Nazi Holocaust of World War II. While imprisoned under deplorable conditions, she and her sister secretly held Bible studies in the barracks. Decades after her release, she wrote a thought-provoking letter in 1974 entitled, *"Prepare for the Coming Tribulation,"* concerning the Pre-Tribulation Rapture doctrine that is taught in many American churches today.

> There are some among us teaching there will be no tribulation, that the Christians will be able to escape all this. In China, the Christians were told, "Don't worry, before the tribulation comes you will be translated –raptured."

Then came a terrible persecution. Millions of Christians were tortured to death. Later I heard a Bishop from China say, sadly, "We have failed. We should have made the people strong for persecution rather than telling them Jesus would come first."

We should be ready for any type of persecution, no matter how great or how small, if it should happen in our lifetime. We can do this by studying the Bible, memorizing scripture, surrendering to God's will, and depending on the Holy Spirit for guidance. We should also take care of and encourage one another.

Jesus said that those who love Him will never experience the wrath of God, but those who desire to live godly lives will suffer persecution in various degrees (2 Timothy 3:12).

If the ultimate sacrifice of life is made, Jesus promised that we will receive a Crown of Life (James 1:12; Revelation 2:10). A crown is a sign of royalty or exalted rank. It is given here to those who possess the qualities of courage and perseverance in the midst of suffering or death.

Jesus said that even if we are mocked or talked about in an evil way, because we follow Him, we should rejoice, because we will be especially blessed in His heavenly kingdom and receive a great reward.

God blesses those who are persecuted for doing right, for the Kingdom of Heaven is theirs. God blesses you when people mock you and persecute you and lie about you and say all sorts of evil things against you because you are my followers. Be happy about it! Be very glad! For a great reward awaits you in heaven (Matthew 5:10-12 NLT).

The Stage is Set

Before a stage production begins, players are chosen and they practice their parts, as the scenery and props are put into place. If we compare this staging to current events, we can see that in the last few decades, the players and stage are already in place for prophecy to be fulfilled right now.

Global leaders are the actors and the world is the stage. The red carpet has been rolled out and the curtains are drawn. The dress rehearsal has been taking place during the pandemic, to gauge public response to radical changes and mandates. Countries are moving into position. The global religious system is waiting in the wings. The stage is set.

The Great Reset that will change the world is finalizing their plans. Its target date to be in place is the year 2030. One detail yet to come is our entrance ticket to participate in this worldwide production.

The ticket? An electronic ID, implanted in a person's hand that will be tied to their bank account. This coming global economic system is in the works right now. There will come a day that without this ID, people will not be able to function in life. This is because they will not be able to buy or sell anything without it.

When we look at the final scene that plays out, it is important to know that the last days' prophecies were viewed from the Middle Eastern or Israeli vantage point with Jerusalem often at its center. Israel is the crossroad to Europe, Asia, and Africa. It is the focal point of all Christ and the prophets taught, since the beginning of time until the end times.

From this Middle Eastern perspective, men of God spoke of future events concerning nearby countries, and possibly even the United States. One of the reasons it is important to understand that the visions were given with the Israeli (Middle Eastern) perspective is because directional terms were often used in the Bible to describe countries that will align against Israel in the future.

The Last Days can refer to the time after Christ ascended into heaven up to the present time, but it usually refers to specific events that will take place seven years before His return.

Past Prophecies Fulfilled

Beginning in Genesis, prophecies were written concerning the coming Messiah who would save people from their sins. There are too many Bible references concerning His first coming to include in this book, but I will mention a few to prove the accuracy of past prophecies and how they all came true. The purpose of this is not only to show that Jesus is the Messiah, but also to prove that since past prophecies all came to fulfillment, it stands to reason that future prophecies will also happen as well.

Thousands of years ago, the prophets, Jesus, and the apostles wrote or spoke about things that are happening in the world today and things that will happen in the future. There is no other explanation as to how they could have accurately described events we see unfolding, except through the power of the Holy Spirit, as God revealed this knowledge to them.

But why should we believe this or Jesus or the prophets? After all, some of the visions seem pretty far-fetched. We know that there is historical evidence concerning Jesus' birth, life, and death, but what about His deity and the details and miracles concerning His life that cannot be swept away as coincidental?

Before we can believe future prophecies, we must validate that both Old Testament prophecies and prophecies spoken by Jesus himself were indeed fulfilled during His lifetime. These events that came true give credibility to Bible prophecy. The first reference is the prediction. The second is the fulfillment.

God would send His Son to earth in human form to save us (Psalm 2:7 / John 3:16-18).

The Messiah (Jesus) would be born of a virgin (Isaiah 7:14 / Luke 1:26, 27, 30, 31).

He would be born in Bethlehem (Micah 5:2 / Luke 2:4, 5, 7).

He would be called out of Egypt (Hosea 11:1 / Matthew 2:14, 15).

He would ride into Jerusalem on a donkey (Zechariah 9:9 / Matthew 21:1-7).

He would be betrayed by a friend (Psalm 41:9 / Luke 22:48).

He would be sold for thirty pieces of silver (Zechariah 11:12 / Matthew 26:15).

He would be silent to his accusers (Isaiah 53:7 / Mark 15:4, 5).

He would be spit upon and beaten (Isaiah 50:6 / Matthew 26:67).

He would be sacrificed for our sins (Isaiah 53:5 / John 11:49-52).

He would have no broken bones in death (Psalm 34:20 / John 19:33).

He would be pierced in death (Zechariah 12:10 / John 19:34).

He would be buried in a rich man's tomb (Isaiah 53:9 / Matthew 27:57-60).

He would be resurrected (Psalm 16:10 / Mark 16:6, 7).

He would ascend to God (Psalm 68:18 / Mark 16:19; Acts 1:9).

ALL of these prophecies were fulfilled in Jesus. Not only these and more, but also the ones Jesus prophesied concerning Peter and himself.

Jesus prophesied that Peter would deny him three times. He even told Peter when he would deny Him. And it happened just that way (Matthew 26:34).

Jesus prophesied that Peter would be martyred by crucifixion, and it happened just that way (John 21:18).

Jesus predicted his own death and third-day resurrection, and it happened just that way (Matthew 17:22-23; Mark 10:33; Luke 18:32-33; John 2:19). This prophecy alone should be proof in itself that everything else Jesus said will also come to pass.

No other religion has ever had their leader make such bold statements or incredible claims, nor physically rise from the dead. **The atoning death for sin and the physical resurrection of Jesus Christ is the distinct difference between Christianity and all other religions.** Take the resurrection out of the equation and you have just another sect. An impotent faith with no hope of eternal life. The Bible says, *If Christ is not risen, your faith is futile; you are still in your sins!* (1 Corinthians 15:17).

There's more. In approximately 30 A.D., the disciples asked Jesus about the future. Christ said that the temple would be destroyed and left in a pile of ruins. He said, *There shall not be left here one stone upon another, that shall not be thrown down* (Matthew 24:2).

This prophecy came true in 70 A.D. when Roman soldiers destroyed and burned the temple in order to melt the gold that was overlaid on the walls. As the gold melted, the soldiers tore the stones apart to gather the gold that had seeped between the cracks, thus fulfilling the prophecy.

These are impressive prophecies to fulfillment ratios. The Bible stands alone in this predictive track record, because 100% of the past prophecies foretelling Jesus' coming to earth, dying on the cross, and rising from the dead have been fulfilled. Not partially, but fully-fulfilled.

Therefore, it is a logical assumption and stands to reason that with the fulfillment of past prophecies, credibility has been established that future prophecies will also be fulfilled.

The Last Days Prophecies of Jesus

Now as He [Jesus] *sat on the Mount of Olives, the disciples came to Him privately, saying, "Tell us, when will these things be? And what will be the sign of Your coming, and of the end of the age?"*

And Jesus answered and said to them: "Take heed that no one deceives you. For many will come in My name, saying, 'I am the Christ,' and will deceive many. And you will hear of wars and rumors of wars. And there will be famines, pestilences, and earthquakes in various places. All these are the beginning of sorrows or birth pangs.

"Then they will deliver you up to tribulation and kill you, and you will be hated by all nations for My name's sake. And then many will be offended, will betray one another, and will hate one another. Then many false prophets will rise up and deceive many. And because lawlessness (sin) *will abound, the love of many will grow cold"* (Matthew 24:3-12).

We see this hatred, betrayal, and persecution of Christians happening world-wide like never before. Jesus even said that the time will come that whoever kills you will think that he's doing God's service (John 16:2). Jesus then repeats the warning about the false prophets (teachers and preachers) again by saying that before He returns, violence will be rampant and the love of sin will take the place of love for God and other people.

Ironically, all this upheaval will create a revival when people realize that they are living in the midst of prophesied events. Many will then turn to Christ and be converted.

This gospel of the kingdom will be preached in all the world as a witness to all the nations, and then the end will come (Matthew 24:14).

Never before in the history of humanity has it been possible to fulfill this prophecy. Prior to this time, missionaries traveled to remote countries to preach the gospel. Some still travel and live amid indigenous people in an attempt to share the Gospel, but since the advent of the Internet this is all changing. Christian websites, social media, GodTube, and YouTube are reaching those who previously were unreachable.

At least fifty-eight African countries now have Internet access. The total average of all African online accessibility has experienced an 11,567% growth in 20 years (Africa Internet Users, 2020 Population and Facebook Statistics).

The numbers grow every day, as the World Economic Forum works to bring Internet connectivity to the rest of Africa, Latin America, and eventually everywhere in the world.

Before the Internet, this prophecy could not have been fulfilled. Now, a person can read the Bible on an app, or hear the Word of God online around the world at any given time of the day or night.

Jesus then tells us what will take place when the Abomination of Desolation occurs. (This is when the Antichrist claims to be God.) Christ warns his followers a third time not to be deceived. He drives this point home again, because the deception will be so subtle, and yet so great that even His own chosen people will be at risk of being fooled.

For false christs and false prophets will rise and show great signs and wonders to deceive, if possible, even the elect (Matthew 24:24).

Deception was the first tool Satan used in the Garden of Eden and he is still wielding it today. He does this by twisting the Truth ever so slightly, so the change is barely noticeable or simply overlooked. When the defining line of Truth is slowly moved in small increments, the new way of believing is gradually tolerated and then accepted, while the traditional way of believing is condemned and then rejected.

Satan quoted God's word to Eve, but he left something out. Eve quoted God's word to the serpent, but she added something in. This misquoting of the Word is happening in the world today, and just like Eve, people are being deceived.

There is a great darkness descending upon many Christians, because they are not using the lamp of God's Word to discern Truth from error. The Bible gives us a stark warning: *My people are destroyed for lack of knowledge* (Hosea 4:6).

Jesus wraps up His discourse with a description of His return and the rapture: *"Immediately after the tribulation of those days the **sun will be darkened, and the moon will***

34

not give its light; the stars will fall from heaven, and the powers of the heavens will be shaken. *Then the sign of the Son of Man will appear in heaven, and then all the tribes of the earth will mourn, and they will see the Son of Man coming on the clouds of heaven with power and great glory. And He will send His angels with a great sound of a trumpet, and they will gather together His elect from the four winds, from one end of heaven to the other* (Matthew 24:29-31).

These events coincide with the **sixth seal** in Revelation, which is also the return of Jesus Christ. *I looked when He opened the sixth seal, and behold, there was a great earthquake; and the **sun became black** as sackcloth of hair, and **the moon became like blood**. And **the stars of heaven fell** to the earth, as a fig tree drops its late figs when it is **shaken** by a mighty wind.* The sky recedes, mountains crumble, and islands disappear. Then the people who were left behind, *hid themselves in the caves and in the rocks of the mountains* and begged the rocks to fall on them, to hide them from the face of God and the wrath of the Lamb (Revelation 6:12-17).

Jesus then describes the rapture as being like it was in the days of Noah, where the separation came quickly while people were going about their daily business, unaware of their impending glory or doom: So will *the coming of the Son of Man be. Two men will be in the field: one will be taken and the other left. Two women will be grinding at the mill: one will be taken and the other left* (Matthew 24:37-41).

The Rebirth of Israel

Now learn this parable from the fig tree: When its branch has already become tender and puts forth leaves, you know that summer is near. So you also, when you see all these things, know that it is near—at the doors! Assuredly, I say to you, this generation will by no means pass away till all these things take place (Matt 24:32-34).

One of the most significant prophecies that Jesus foretold has been fulfilled during this past generation, which is the rebirth of the nation of Israel. The end time prophetic clock began ticking when this event occurred.

After Jerusalem was invaded and Herod's Temple was destroyed in 70 A.D., the Jewish people were scattered all over the known world, and Gentiles (non-Jews) occupied the land for nearly 2,000 years.

On May 14, 1948, the state of Israel was given back to the Jews and it was recognized as their country again. The Jewish people flowed back into their homeland from all over the world, thus fulfilling the prophecy:

I will bring your descendants from the east, and gather you from the west; I will say to the north, 'Give them up!' and to the south, 'Do not keep them back!' Bring My sons from afar, and My daughters from the ends of the earth (Isaiah 43:5-6).

Isaiah not only tells us how quickly this will happen, but he also mentions Jerusalem (Zion) by name, confirming that this prophecy is indeed about Israel:

Who has ever seen anything as strange as this? Who ever heard of such a thing? Has a nation ever been born in a single day? Has a country ever come forth in a mere moment? But by the time Jerusalem's birth pains begin, her children will be born (Isaiah 66:8 NLT).

Jesus also said, *"Jerusalem shall be trodden down of the Gentiles until the times of the Gentiles be fulfilled"* (Luke 21:24b).

This prophecy came to pass in 1967 with the establishment of Jerusalem after the six-day war. Then, on May 14, 2018, President Trump declared Jerusalem the capital of Israel on the 70th anniversary of Israel becoming a nation.

The regathering and establishing of Israel as a nation and Jerusalem being its capital has been fulfilled as prophesied. This may be what Jesus was referring to when He mentioned the budding of the fig tree. If this is the case then the generation of people who see this event will be the ones who witness the calamities spoken of in Matthew and the return of Jesus Christ (24:34).

What is The Falling Away?

*Now, brethren, **concerning the coming of our Lord Jesus Christ and our gathering together to Him**, we ask you, not to be soon shaken in mind or troubled, either by spirit or by word or by letter, as if from us, as though **the day of Christ had come*** (2 Thessalonians 2:1-2).

Some Christians in the early church believed that the rapture had already taken place and they had missed it, so Paul was setting them straight by telling them that it will be a future event, and two things must first take place before the rapture happens and the Lord returns.

*Let no one deceive you by any means; for **that Day will not come unless***:
  (1) *The falling away comes first.*
  (2) *That man of sin is revealed, the son of perdition who opposes and exalts himself above all that is called God or that is worshiped, so that he sits as God in the temple of God, showing himself that he is God* (2 Thessalonians 2:3-4).

"That Day" or the "Day of the Lord" always refers to the Second Coming of Jesus Christ when He returns to rid the world of evil at the battle at Armageddon. The original

Greek word *hēmera*w confirms that this is referring to *"The day Christ will return from heaven, raise the dead, hold the final judgment, and perfect his kingdom"* (Strong's 2250). Therefore, the falling away and the revealing of the man of sin take place before that time.

- *But of **that day** and hour no one knows, not even the angels of heaven, but My Father only* (Matthew 24:36).

- *I say to you that it will be more tolerable in **that Day** for Sodom than for that city* (Luke 10:12).

- *Take heed to yourselves, lest your hearts be weighed down with carousing, drunkenness, and cares of this life, and **that Day** come on you unexpectedly* (Luke 21:34).

- *The sun shall be turned into darkness, and the moon into blood, before the coming of the great and awesome **day of the Lord*** (Acts 2:20).

- *For you yourselves know perfectly that **the day of the Lord** so comes as a thief in the night* (1 Thessalonians 5:2).

- *But **the day of the Lord** will come as a thief in the night, in which the heavens will pass away with a great noise, and the elements will melt with fervent heat; both the earth and the works that are in it will be burned up* (2 Peter 3:10).

The falling away or apostasy will happen before the Antichrist is revealed. We have seen this desertion of the basic principles of Christianity more than ever in the past few decades. This blatant neglect, rejection, and rebellion of Biblical Truths stems from deception, temptation or persecution, or simply because people want to believe their own version of truth and do what is right in their own eyes. The Bible has something to say about this: *There is a way that seems right to a man, but its end is the way of death* (Proverbs 14:12).

In the latter times some will depart from the faith, giving heed to deceiving spirits and doctrines of demons, speaking lies in hypocrisy, having their own conscience seared with a hot iron (1 Timothy 4:1).

In the last days perilous times will come: For men will be lovers of themselves, lovers of money...[and] *lovers of pleasure rather than lovers of God,* **having a form of godliness** but denying its power (2 Timothy 3:1-5).

The beast will then be unleashed. *He who now restrains will do so until He is taken **out of the way**. And then the lawless one will be revealed, whom the Lord will consume with the breath of His mouth and destroy with the brightness of His coming* (2 Thessalonians 2:6-8).

Many of those who adhere to a pre-tribulation rapture stance believe that the restrainer is the Holy Spirit, and that He is the one taken *out of the way* when the rapture happens, which is a possibility, but very unlikely.

The illogical part to this stance is that if the Holy Spirit leaves the earth, how will people be converted and saved when the two witnesses preach and do miracles, since it is the Holy Spirit who does the work of regeneration and empowers these believers to do divine wonders? (Revelation 11:3, 6).

The Spirit must also be here to empower people to refuse the Mark of the Beast. Without the Holy Spirit's help, many would not have the strength to resist and would succumb to the Mark due to fear of death or lack of basic necessities.

Upon further investigation, "the way" (as in taken out of the way) can be translated, "the middle" (Strong's G3319). Therefore, this "taken out of the way" could mean that the Holy Spirit steps aside from center stage, rather than completely leaves the earth (since that does not scripturally make sense).

This also could mean that the world will be so evil during this time, that the Holy Spirit will be quenched to such a degree that there is little evidence of His presence. The fruit of love, joy, peace, patience, gentleness, kindness, goodness, faithfulness or self-control will be greatly lacking at that time (Galatians 5:22-23).

This falling away may also mean a falling away from the one true faith in Jesus Christ, His blood atonement for sin on the Cross, and His subsequent resurrection. This teaching is missing in many churches today, thus the Holy Spirit who convicts a soul of sin and indwells a person upon conversion is absent from those places too (John 16:8).

The stage is being set for the Antichrist to be welcomed with open arms, a "strong delusion" comes upon many people. The Bible says, *The coming of the lawless one [the Antichrist] is according to the working of Satan, with all power, signs, and lying wonders, and with all unrighteous*

41

*deception among those who perish, **because they did not receive the love of the truth, that they might be saved**. And for this reason God will send them a **strong delusion, that they should believe the lie**, that they all may be condemned **who did not believe the truth but had pleasure in unrighteousness*** (2 Thessalonians 2:9-11).

Delusion is a very strong word, yet there it is. When people are deluded they believe things that are not real or true. In psychology, delusion is classified as a mental disorder, and yet we are seeing signs of delusion in the world today. "Good is evil. Evil is good. Truth is a lie. Lies are the truth." Spiritual and natural truths and absolutes are being torn down while sin is built up and accepted as normal.

We need not look very far to see the lies that people believe and the evil that is called good or normal. The prophet Isaiah warned of this delusion hundreds of years before Christ was born when he said, *Woe to those who call evil good, and good evil; who put darkness for light, and light for darkness* (Isaiah 5:20).

The deception and delusions will become more prevalent the closer we get to the Lord's return. *For the time will come when they will not endure sound doctrine, but according to their own desires, because they have itching ears, they will heap up for themselves teachers; and **they will turn their ears away from the truth, and be turned aside to fables*** (2 Timothy 4:3-4).

Ministers who preach a prosperity gospel add another deception to the mix. This form of idolatry goes against what Jesus told his followers and the Pharisees, which was they cannot serve God and chase after money (Luke 16:13-15). Jesus never told people how to get rich while they lived here on earth, but rather how to store up eternal treasures for when they get to heaven (Matthew 6:19-20).

Jesus said, *"The Spirit of the Lord is upon Me, because He has anointed Me to preach the gospel to the poor."* Not to preach prosperity to the poor (Luke 4:18).

Another campaign of deception is when people twist the Scriptures to fit what *they* believe. One of the biggest lies is humanism or universalism. This belief omits the concept of sin by saying, "Everyone is a child of God and therefore going to heaven." Logic clearly infers that this is not the case, because if this were true then people like Hitler, Stalin, Nero, mass murderers, and the vilest of pedophiles and predators would be in heaven.

If Jesus told the average person with minimal sins (comparatively), *"Unless you repent you will all likewise perish,"* how much more should repentance be in order for the foulest of them all? (Luke 13:5).

God is holy and just and cannot look upon sin no matter how great or how small, nor can he tolerate it to any degree (Habakkuk 1:13). Repentance turns our hearts to God, and because of His great love for us, He made a way to reconcile sinners to Himself, and repentance is the first step.

The next step is believing that Jesus is the Son of God who came to earth to forgive our sins and give us eternal life. He was crucified, died, buried, and then rose from the dead, so we can have peace with God and live with Him forever in heaven (1 Corinthians 15:3-4). This transaction sets us free from the sentence of death and restores our relationship with God.

Humanism assumes we are all good to go, but provides no proof as to where we are going, nor precise way to get there, nor how to approach a perfect and holy God. As much as many people don't want to believe it, the Bible clearly says that without Christ as Savior, we are *not* children of God. On the contrary, the scriptures tell us that we are children of wrath, spiritually dead in sin, and enemies of God, and the only solution is salvation through Christ.

- *"Most assuredly, I* (Jesus) *say to you, unless one is **born again**, he cannot see the kingdom of God. For God did not send His Son into the world to condemn the world, but that the world through Him might be **saved**. He who believes in Him is not condemned; but **he who does not believe is condemned already**, because he has not believed in the name of the only begotten Son of God"* (John 3:3, 17-18).

- *And you He made alive, who were **dead in trespasses and sins**, in which you once walked according to the course of this world, according to the prince of the power of the air* (Satan), *the spirit who now works in the **sons of disobedience**, among whom also we all once conducted ourselves in the lusts of our flesh, fulfilling the desires of the flesh and of the mind, **and were by nature children of wrath, just as the others**.*

  *But God, who is rich in mercy, because of His great love with which He loved us, even **when we were dead in trespasses**, made us **alive together with Christ, by grace you have been saved*** (Ephesians 2:1-5).

- *God demonstrates His own love toward us, in that while we were still sinners, Christ died for us. Much more then, having now been justified by His blood, we shall be saved from wrath through Him. For if **when we were enemies we were reconciled to God through the death of His Son,** much more, having been reconciled, we shall be saved by His life* (Romans 5:6, 8-10).

The Good News is this gift of salvation is free to all who repent and receive Christ as Savior. It is through the new birth that we become a part of God's family.

- ***As many as received Him*** *(Jesus), to them He gave the right to become children of God, to those who believe in His name* (John 1:12-13).

- *For **whoever does the will of My Father** in heaven is My brother and sister and mother* (Matthew 12:50; Mark 3:35).

- *My mother and My brothers are these **who hear the word of God and do it*** (Luke 8:21).

- *For you are all children of God **through faith in Christ Jesus*** (Galatians 3:26).

First the deception and then the delusion. We must not be fooled. We must compare everything we hear or read with the Word of God.

How Will We Recognize the Antichrist?

The previous chapter covered one of the two events that must take place *"concerning **the coming of our Lord Jesus Christ and our gathering together to Him***" (2 Thessalonians 2:1).

The second part to this prophecy is *"that man of sin is revealed, the son of perdition who opposes and exalts himself above all that is called God or that is worshiped, so that he sits as God in the temple of God, showing himself that he is God"* (2 Thessalonians 2:3-4).

The signing of the peace treaty between Israel and the Antichrist will mark the beginning of Daniel's 70th week, which will set in motion the seven year Tribulation period. Although the Antichrist will be on the scene for the signing of the peace agreement, we may not know for sure who he is at that time, because there will be many people involved in the process.

A period of seventy sets of seven (490 years) *has been decreed for your people and your holy city to finish their rebellion, to put an end to their sin, to atone for their guilt, to bring in everlasting righteousness, to confirm the prophetic vision, and to anoint the Most Holy Place.*

After this period of sixty-two sets of seven (483 years) ***the Anointed One*** (Jesus) ***will be killed, appearing to have*** *accomplished nothing, and a ruler will arise whose armies will destroy the city and the Temple. The end will come with a flood, and war and its miseries are decreed from that time to the very end* (Daniel 9:24-26 NLT).

This prophecy was fulfilled when Jesus was crucified and died. The temple was later destroyed in 70 A.D. There is a 2,000 year gap between the death of Christ and the latter part of this prophecy. The final "week" of testing is yet to come.

The (Last Days) *ruler will make a treaty with the people for a period of one set of seven. After half this time, he will put an end to the sacrifices and offerings* [in Jerusalem]. *And as a climax to all his terrible deeds, he will set up a sacrilegious object that causes desecration, until the fate decreed for this defiler is finally poured out on him* (Daniel 9:27).

People will know who the Antichrist is when he breaks the peace covenant with Israel 3 ½ years after the initial signing of the treaty. This is when there will be no doubt who the Antichrist is, because he will set himself up in the holy place, declare that he is god (the messiah or savior), and require that he be obeyed and worshiped.

This blasphemous event marks the middle of the Tribulation period. At this point, life on earth dramatically changes for Christians. *There will be a time of anguish greater than any since nations first came into existence* (Daniel 12:1b).

The Bible says, *This man* (the Antichrist) *will come to do the work of Satan with counterfeit power and signs and miracles. He will use every kind of evil deception to fool* *those on their way to destruction, because **they refuse to love and accept the truth that would save them*** (2 Thessalonians 2:9-10 NLT).

Why is the Peace Treaty with Israel Important?

[The Antichrist] *shall confirm a covenant **with many** for one week,* or seven years (Daniel 9:27).

I looked up and saw a white horse standing there. Its rider carried a bow, and a crown was placed on his head. He rode out to win many battles and gain the victory (Revelation 6:2).

The Antichrist is the rider on the white horse when the first seal in Revelation is opened. He carries a bow, but no arrows, which seems to indicate that his victories are won through peace and persuasion (at the beginning of his rule). He wears white like the righteous and a crown like a king, which makes him appear to be a good leader.

This prophecy coincides with Daniel's vision, *And through his policy also he shall cause craft to prosper in his hand; and **he shall magnify himself in his heart,** and **by peace shall destroy many*** (Daniel 8:25 KJV).

On December 6, 2017, former President Trump made an historic declaration that Jerusalem is the "One and Only Capital of the Jewish State of Israel." On May 14, 2018, the

United States officially opened its Embassy in Jerusalem (exactly 70 years after Israel became a nation again).

This makes it possible for a temple to be built there at some future date. This is important because a temple is necessary to fulfill the prophecy of the Antichrist entering the holy sanctuary and declaring that he is God (the Messiah).

[The Antichrist] *opposes and exalts himself above all that is called God or that is worshiped, so that he sits as God in the temple of God, showing himself that he is God* (2 Thessalonians 2:4).

In order for the temple to be built, there must be peace and permission to build it on the Temple Mount. The problem is that it is currently the site of the Dome of the Rock and the Al Aqsa mosque, which are places of Gentile (non-Jewish) worship.

We also know there will be some form of a temple on site because in his vision, John is told to measure it: *Then I was given a reed like a measuring rod. And the angel stood, saying, "Rise and measure the temple of God, the altar, and those who worship there. But **leave out the court which is outside the temple, and do not measure it, for it has been given to the Gentiles**. And they will tread the holy city underfoot for forty-two months"* (Revelation 11:1-2). The holy city always refers to Jerusalem.

The Tribulation timeline begins and hinges on Israel signing the Peace Treaty with neighboring countries. (Palestine will most likely be the hinge-pin that sets things in motion). Under former President Trump's leadership, Jared Kushner authored the peace plan that led to four Middle

Eastern countries normalizing ties with Israel. The Abrahamic Peace Accord recognizes that Jews, Christians and Muslims share the same ancestral father, Abraham. Although this is true, one group in this trio is not part of God's covenant of promise. The Muslim lineage is from Ishmael, and he was not the chosen son through which the redeemer would be born.

Nevertheless, this is the common thread that leaders are weaving together at the peace treaty table. It may also be the unifying factor that will allow them to all freely worship on the Temple Mount. The United States administration often calls these treaties, "normalization agreements."

Many leaders will be involved in the future signing of this peace pact, which may be an extension to the Abrahamic Accord. The key signers who set things in motion may come from any of Israel's surrounding countries who are at odds with her, but it will most likely be signed by leaders from Palestine and / or leaders of the European Union.

The Bible states that after the first 3 ½ years of the Tribulation, the global leader will declare that he is the messiah (savior). When this happens, life on earth will take a dramatic turn for the worse.

This will begin the time of terror and the dividing line between faithful Christians and non-believers. The choice of who people pledge their allegiance to at this time, will reveal their faith in Christ or lack thereof. This decision will seal their fate and determine their eternal destination.

The Four Great Divisions of People

As an introduction to the rapture for those who may not know, the Bible records two divisions in the past that separated God's people from the unrepentant and unbelieving. The Bible also records that there will be two great divisions in the future that will separate Christians from the unfaithful, unrepentant and unbelieving.

The first localized divisions took place during the time of Lot. Before God judged Sodom and Gomorrah, an angel told Lot and his family to run for their lives and not look back, because the cities would be destroyed by fire and brimstone (Genesis 19). Lot and his family were saved by grace, but acted in faith by running away in order to receive the promise.

The saving of Rahab and her family when Jericho fell was also a localized division. They were saved by grace, but acted in faith by hanging a scarlet rope from the window and staying inside their home in order to receive the promise (Joshua 2:18).

The second worldwide division occurred during the time of Noah. Before God judged the world, He told Noah what was going to happen and how to prepare for the flood. Noah and his family believed God and followed His instructions by building the ark. The eight were saved by grace, but acted in faith by building the ark and then getting inside in order to receive the promise (Genesis 6-:11-22).

The third division between heaven and earth will take place at the rapture. This snatching away will separate the faithful in Christ from the unbelieving and the unfaithful. Jesus will base His decision by the fruit that he sees (or lack thereof), as evidence of genuine faith and conversion (Matthew 7:21; 18:3-4; 25:1-13).

We are saved by grace through faith in Christ, but we must repent to receive the promise. Many people do not believe that repentance is a prerequisite to salvation, but this command is found throughout the Bible, and it is mentioned over fifty times in the New Testament alone.

Repentance is a change of attitude concerning sin and the turning away from it in one's mind. The Bible says, *For godly sorrow produces repentance leading to salvation* (2 Corinthians 7:10).

The first message that John the Baptist and Jesus both preached was, *"Repent, for the kingdom of heaven is at hand!"* (Matthew 3:2; 4:17).

- Jesus preached about the kingdom of God, and said, *Repent and believe the gospel* (Mark 1:14-15).

- Jesus later said, *Repent or you will perish.* He also said, *I have not come to call* [those who think they are] *righteous, but sinners, to repentance* (Luke 5:32; 13:3).

- The last command that Jesus gave to his followers before he ascended into heaven was that *Repentance and remission of sins should be preached in His name to all nations* (Luke 24:47).

- The first sermon that Peter preached commanded the people to repent: *Repent, and let every one of you be baptized in the name of Jesus Christ for the remission of sins; and you shall receive the gift of the Holy Spirit* (Acts 2:38).

- The final warning Jesus gave **five of the seven churches** in Revelation was, *"Repent"* (Revelation 2:5, 16, 21-22; 3:3, 19).

The last time repentance is mentioned in the Bible is during the Tribulation and concerns those who refuse to do so, and therefore they are doomed (Revelation 9:20-21; 16:9-11).

Repentance is clearly a biblical teaching and it is a prerequisite to the gift of salvation. It is also an ongoing process in our journey to become like Christ. A lack of this teaching leads to powerless preaching, defeated Christians, and non-converted congregations.

The fourth division between heaven and hell is when Jesus separates those who wanted nothing to do with Him or His Word by granting their request. Therefore, they will have nothing to do with Him or His promises for all eternity.

This division will take place at the Great White Throne Judgment. The unbelieving, the unloving, the arrogant, the greedy, the immoral, the self-righteous, and the evil will stand before Christ to be judged based on how they lived their lives (Revelation 21:8).

These are the ones who did not want a Savior and mediator on earth, so they will be judged without one on that day in the heavenly court.

And just as it is in our courts of law, those without a lawyer to defend them or a whipping-boy, scapegoat, or fall guy to take their place, they will suffer the verdict and punishment themselves. Thus, by their own choosing, these willful ones are destined to spend eternity in the Lake that burns with Fire (Matthew 25:41-46; Revelation 20:11-15).

Jesus said, *"If you do not believe that I AM* [the Savior], *you will die in your sins"* (John 8:24).

The Days of Noah | The Door Was Shut

Jesus said, *"I am the door. If anyone enters by Me, he will be saved"* (John 10:9).

As it was in the days of Noah, so it will be also in the days of the Son of Man. [And] *on the day that Lot went out of Sodom it rained fire and brimstone from heaven and destroyed them all. Even so will it be in the day when the Son of Man is revealed* (Luke 17:26, 29-30).

Jesus said that when he returns, life will be like it was in the days of Noah and Lot. When Noah was alive, the earth was filled with corruption and violence.

Although these things are in the world today, Jesus was also referring to the suddenness of His return. He said it would come like lightning and unexpectedly like the flood in the days of Noah and the fire in the days of Lot.

During both times, people were living life as usual, eating, drinking and getting married. Then one day the flood came and swept them all away. And then one day the fire rained down and burned them all away (Genesis 6:5, 11; 19:24-25).

Jesus compared these two events to how the world will be before He returns: They were not only immoral, ungodly and violent, but they were distracted, unrepentant and unconcerned.

In one day the flood came while Noah was safely in the ark. **In one day** Lot left town then the fire and brimstone rained down. *Even so will it be* **in the day** *when the Son of Man is revealed* (Luke 17:26-30).

Jesus said that His return will be visible and sudden like lightning. *As the lightning that flashes out of one part under heaven shines to the other part under heaven, so also the Son of Man will be* **in His day** (Luke 17:24).

Christians will be removed before God's wrath is poured out. The following description of daily activities indicate that the rapture will happen quickly before Christ returns.

In those days before the flood, the people were enjoying banquets and parties and weddings right up to the time Noah entered his boat. People didn't realize what was going to happen until the flood came and swept them all away. ***That is the way it will be when the Son of Man comes.*** *Then* ***two men will be in the field:*** *one will be taken and the other left. Two women will be grinding at the mill:* ***one will be taken and the other left.*** *Watch therefore, for* *you do not know what hour your Lord is coming* (Matthew 24:38-42 NLT).

Yet, the people in Noah's day knew something dramatic was going to happen. It's hard to miss a man building a boat for 120 years and not wonder what's going on. They had no knowledge of rain, because the earth was watered by a mist back then, so they would not have thought that a flood was coming. There were also no bodies of water nearby, nor any way to move the ark if there was a place to float it (Genesis 6:13-20).

They were warned by Noah, the preacher of righteousness, that something dramatic was going to happen, but they did not believe him (2 Peter 2:5). There was a way to be saved, but in order to do so, they would have had to leave their former life behind and walk through the door of the ark.

Anyone who has experienced a tsunami or watched a video of one taking place knows how quickly things can escalate. Cars and houses are carried away. Trees are ripped up by their roots. People run for their lives to find high places. Death, disaster and destruction ensue.

Yet, before the tidal wave occurs there are always signs. An earthquake off shore and water receding from the beach are two huge indicators that disaster is imminent. Those who pay attention to the signs have a better chance of running and surviving than those who ignore the obvious.

During the time of the worldwide flood, it wasn't a tsunami. The water came fast and furious from *every direction at once*. The rain not only fell down in a deluge when the windows of heaven opened, but oceans and seas shot up like geysers when the crust of the earth broke up (Genesis 7:11).

And it came to pass after seven days that the waters of the flood were on the earth. In the six hundredth year of Noah's life, in the second month, the seventeenth day of the month, **on that day** *all the fountains of the great deep were broken up, and the windows of heaven were opened. And the Lord shut him in* (Genesis 7:10-11, 16b).

Right up until the time Noah entered the ark, people were eating and drinking and getting married. They did not pay attention to the most glaring sign they had seen for over one-hundred years: A man and his family building a boat.

This intentional obliviousness happened in Noah's day and it's happening again today, as prophetic signs are unfolding before our very eyes. And just like those in Noah's day, people don't want to believe it's true.

When the rain fell down and the waters rose up, it was too late to get on board. God had shut the door the week before with Noah and his family tucked safely inside, while those outside perished (Genesis 7:4).

In one day everything changed. Life came to a halt for everyone except the eight people and the animals inside the ark. The Lord shut the door, and once it closed no one else could get inside, no matter how hard they tried or how loud they cried.

One day, everything will change. It will be the same lightning speed scenario when the Lord returns and shuts the door (Matthew 24:37-39).

The Ten Virgins | The Door was Shut

Jesus compared the kingdom of heaven to ten virgins who took their lamps and went out to meet the bridegroom. Five of them were wise because they had oil in their lamps, and five of them were foolish because they did not have enough oil.

*"And at midnight a cry was heard: 'Behold, the bridegroom is coming; go out to meet him!' Then all those virgins arose and trimmed their lamps. And the foolish said to the wise, '**Give us some of your oil, for our lamps are going out.**' But the wise answered, saying, 'No, lest there should not be enough for us and you; but go rather to those who sell, and buy for yourselves.' And while they went to buy, the bridegroom came, and **those who were ready went in with him** to the wedding; **and the door was shut*** (Matthew 25:1-10).

When we read this passage, we see that the oil was a key factor in determining whether the brides went through the door or not. (The oil will be examined in the next section.)

In historical Jewish engagements, the intended groom would go away for up to two years to prepare a place for his bride and him to live. This is similar to Jesus preparing a place in Heaven before He returns to claim His Bride (the church), to live with Him forever (John 14:2).

In the Jewish culture of that time, if a woman was unfaithful during the engagement period while waiting for the groom, she was sheltered away and did not marry her intended husband.

In a similar way, the unfaithful Christian will be left behind and will not be united with Christ in His kingdom.

*"Afterward the other virgins came also, saying, 'Lord, Lord, open to us!' But he answered and said, 'Assuredly, I say to you, **I do not know you'*** (Matthew 25:11-12).

When the remaining virgins asked the groom (Jesus) to let them in, he did not justify or explain his decision, he simply said, *"I don't know you."* And just as it was in the case of Noah, once the door was shut it would not be opened again, no matter how much pounding or pleading one did.

It's an awful thought to think that people will be left outside the door, because Jesus did not know them. Of course, Jesus knows everyone and everything. What He means here is that there was no relationship between them.

A commitment to Christ can be compared to a traditional marriage between a man and woman. A couple cannot just say, "I do," during the ceremony and then live like they did when they were single. Marriage is meant to be a permanent bond with a lifestyle change that makes fidelity a priority. The evidence of the couple's love will also be expressed in words and deeds. If there is no commitment or interaction there is no real relationship.

We see a similar warning in yet another passage. *Jesus said, "Not everyone who says to Me, 'Lord, Lord,' shall **enter** the kingdom of heaven, **but he who does the will of My Father** in heaven. Many will say to Me **in that day**, 'Lord, Lord, have we not prophesied in Your name, cast out demons in Your name, and done many wonders in Your name?' And then I will declare to them, '**I never knew you**; depart from Me, you who practice lawlessness!'"* (Matthew 7:21, 23).

These people *may be* more concerned with a particular *gift* of the Holy Spirit that glorifies them in the process, rather than the *fruit* of the Holy Spirit that transforms a person from the inside-out and glorifies God in the process (Galatians 5:22-23).

A more "gifted" or "enlightened" spirit of superiority *may* have also seeped into this group. And pride has no place in the kingdom of God. This passage may be referring to false teachers and preachers, but we also see Jesus give this same warning to a stranger, who asked him how many people would be saved.

*"Strive to enter through the narrow gate, for many, I say to you, will seek to enter and will not be able. Once the Master of the house has risen up and **shut the door**, and you begin to stand outside and knock at the door, saying, 'Lord, Lord, open for us,' and He will answer and say to you, '**I do not know you**'"* (Luke 13:23-25).

To understand what Jesus means by him "not knowing" someone, imagine a person saying, "I know the president." That person may try to enter the Oval Office, but he will not be allowed inside unless the president says, "Yes, I know that person." If the president does not know that man, it doesn't matter how much he claims to know the president, or how many details he knows *about* the president, he's leaving with the group when the tour is over.

In the same way, a man or woman may know a lot about Jesus, but still not have a personal relationship with Him. Following Jesus is an act of obedience. Christ even said this himself: *"Why do you call Me 'Lord, Lord,' and not do the things which I say?"* (Luke 6:46).

A passive faith is no faith at all. For as the body without the spirit is dead, so faith without works is dead also (James 2:26).

What Does the Oil Represent?

The foolish (virgins) *said to the wise, 'Give us some of your oil, for our lamps are going out.'* The wise virgins basically said, you must get your own. *And while they went to buy, the bridegroom came, and those who were ready went in with him to the wedding; and the door was shut* (Matthew 25:1-10).

Since the oil or lack thereof was a determining factor in whether the brides went through the door or not, it is imperative that we know what the oil is. To find out, all we need to do is look at other passages that refer to oil and light.

Jesus calls the church lamps in Revelation 1:20. He also used this definition when he told His followers, "*You are the light of the world. Let your light so shine before men, that they may see your good works, and glorify your Father in heaven*" (Matthew 5:14, 16).

A lamp provides light to dispel the dark and helps people see when they walk. As Christians, we are to shine our lights for the world to see Jesus working in and through us, so that they can see the light of Christ and know the way of salvation.

We shine our light by living righteous lives, walking in truth, and loving one another. By sharing a kind smile, by doing good deeds, by meeting the needs of those who cannot fend for themselves. These actions are *evidence* of our salvation and the Spirit working through us (Ephesians 2:10).

Some people believe that the virgins who were left behind were not really saved or they did not have the Holy Spirit. This is not a possibility because the verse says they were all waiting to meet the groom, and they all had some measure of oil in their lamps, but five of them didn't have enough to keep their lamps lit. The five left behind may have been lazy, distracted, double-minded, or half-hearted in their commitment to the groom. And because they were blasé in their faith or unfaithful in their marriage commitment, they did not consider and plan for their future.

So what does the oil represent?

In ancient times, olives were pressed to release their oil, which was then used as fuel, to burn and create light. Olives are fruit, therefore, the oil the virgins had or lacked, represents fruit or what they produced, or did not produce in their lives.

Fruit is evidence of being connected to the vine of Christ (John 15:1-5). The fruit is also a result of the Holy Spirit working through a person to produce the fruit of righteousness and the fruit of the Spirit (Philippians 1:11; Galatians 5:22-23).

If there is no fruit, there is no fire. If there is no fire, there is no light.

Jesus used this fire, light, lamp comparison again when he said, *"Be dressed for **service** and **keep your lamps burning**, as though you were waiting for your master to return from the wedding feast"* (Luke 12:35-36 NLT).

There is a clear correlation between fruit and living righteous lives while doing good deeds for others. The virgins who lacked oil were told to *go buy* some for themselves. Obtaining oil will *cost* us something, as we *spend* our time, energy or resources helping other people and caring for them.

*I, the Lord, search the heart, I test the mind, even to give every man according to his ways, according to the **fruit of his doings*** (Jeremiah 17:10).

Jesus shows love to us by His gift of Grace; We show love to Him by how we treat other people (Matthew 25:40). His mercy and grace create a desire in us to do His will, which then manifests in us a deeper sense of His presence.

"He who has My (Jesus) *commandments and keeps them, it is he who loves Me. And he who loves Me will be loved by My Father, and I will love him and manifest Myself to him."*

"If anyone loves Me, he will keep My word; and My Father will love him, and We will come to him and make Our home with him. He who does not love me does not keep my words (John 14:21, 23-24).

What Does it Mean to Follow Christ?

*The other virgins came also, saying, 'Lord, Lord, open to us!' But he answered and said, 'Assuredly, I say to you, **I do not know you'*** (Matthew 25:11-12)

Contrast the above verse with this one: *My sheep **hear My voice, and I know them,** [because] **they follow Me*** (John 10:10).

Jesus simply said that he "knows them," because they follow Him. Since we cannot physically follow Christ around the city or town where we live, we must look further to see what He means by following Him. It's easy to understand, if we compare this to a person following a guide while hiking.

The trail guide not only shows hikers the way by example, but also warns them of obstacles and dangers. He tells them where to step, where to turn, when to stoop down, and when to climb up. Following this person requires obedience to safely reach the intended destination.

This concept is no different when Jesus said to follow Him. He speaks to us primarily through His Word and through the still small voice of the Holy Spirit, but he also speaks to us by listening in prayer and through other Spirit-filled Christians.

And just like following a trail guide, we must listen and then follow Christ through these means. Obedience to his commands help us steer clear of pitfalls and ditches and cliffs. As we follow His lead, He will take us, not only to green pastures, but also to eternal riches and rewards by-way-of the rugged road that is often difficult, narrow and steep.

Jesus said, "I am the way" (John 14:6). And if we follow in His footsteps and walk in humility, love and Truth, we will be doing the Father's will (1 Peter 2:21; Matthew 16:24).

The Bible says, *He who says he abides in Him ought himself also to walk just as He walked* (1 John 2:6). If we are not showing kindness and compassion to those we have deemed unworthy or beneath us, we're not really following Christ, because he commanded us to love one another. Jesus said that if we withhold love from the "least of these," we are withholding it from him (John 15:12; Matthew 25:45).

A self-righteous, unloving attitude is what Jesus was referring to when he gave the following example.

"Two men went to the Temple to pray. One was a Pharisee, and the other was a despised tax collector. The Pharisee stood by himself and prayed this prayer: 'I thank you, God, that I am not like other people—cheaters, sinners, adulterers. I'm certainly not like that tax collector! I fast twice a week, and I give you a tenth of my income.'

"But the tax collector stood at a distance and dared not even lift his eyes to heaven as he prayed. Instead, he beat his chest in sorrow, saying, 'O God, be merciful to me, for I am a sinner.' I tell you, this sinner, not the Pharisee, returned home justified before God. For those who exalt themselves will be humbled, and those who humble themselves will be exalted" (Luke 18:10-14 NLT).

Again, Jesus makes it clear that He knows those who belong to him. He affirmed this by saying, *My sheep hear my voice, and **I know them, and they follow me**: And I give them eternal life; and they shall never perish; neither shall **anyone** snatch them out of my hand* (John 10:9, 27-28).

Many people use this verse when referring to someone who strays from the Truth or falls into sin, but this is not its meaning. The word *snatch* is translated from the word, *harpazo*, which is the same word used to describe the quick removal of Christians at the rapture. But here it is used to emphasize that **no person** can snatch you from Jesus' hand. Therefore, it is absolutely true that we cannot lose our salvation, nor can anyone take it from us.

All who have a genuine faith in Christ are safely in His hand and no one can snatch them from His grasp, *but* a person can choose to forfeit the gift of salvation and step out of His hand.

One way a person can do this is by willfully walking away from Christ when they choose to live life on their own terms. This happened when a group of Jesus' followers were confused and offended by Christ's sayings, so they walked away and stopped following Him (John 6:60-61).

Therefore many of His **disciples,** *when they heard this, said, "This is a hard saying; who can understand it?" From that time many of* **His disciples went back and walked with Him no more** (John 6:66).

These people were called disciples, but Jesus knew they really didn't believe in Him, and therefore they did not stay with Him (John 6:64). If they were truly His followers, they would have continued to walk with Him.

They went out from us, but they were not of us; for if they had been of us, they would have continued with us; but they went out that they might be made manifest, that none of them were of us (1 John 2:19).

The prodigal son also walked away from his father with thoughts of only pleasing himself. He took up living a wild life and blew his inheritance on parties and prostitutes. When his money ran out and a famine arose, he took a job feeding pigs to survive (Luke 15:13, 15, 30).

As much as the father unconditionally loved his son, he called him "dead" and "lost" when he turned away, left home, and chose to willfully live in sin.

The father then said his son was "alive" and "found" when the son repented and returned to him (Luke 15:24, 32). The father didn't care how ragged and dirty his son was when he suddenly showed up one day. The father freely forgave and cleaned him up without question or hesitation.

Yet, as much as the father loved the son and wanted to be with him, the son could not come into the house if he brought the hogs and harlots with him. He had to be willing to leave his sinful lifestyle behind in order to come inside (Luke 15:18). There was also a mutual understanding that he would not travel back and forth between these two worlds.

The father in this story represents God the Father in heaven, who responds the same way. *God, who is rich in mercy, because of His great love with which He loved us, even when we were dead in trespasses, made us alive together with Christ (by grace you have been saved)* (Ephesians 2:4, 5).

We also see this example in the life of Christ when He did not allow sin in His Father's house. He cleansed the temple by flipping tables and driving the money-changers out with a whip (John 2:15). Christ did not tolerate or make allowance for sin, He made a way for us to be free from it. When we repent and come to Christ, He cleans us up and sets our feet on the right path.

This topic of walking away was also addressed by the Apostle Peter. *When people escape from the wickedness of the world by knowing our Lord and Savior Jesus Christ and then get tangled up and enslaved by sin again, they are worse off than before.*

*It would be better if they had never known the way to righteousness than to know it and then **reject** the command they were given to live a holy life. They prove the truth of this proverb: "A dog returns to its vomit."And another says, "A washed pig returns to the mud"* (2 Peter 2:20-22 NLT).

James, the half-brother of Jesus, also warned believers. ***Brethren****, if anyone **among you** wanders from the truth, and someone turns him back, let him know that he who **turns a sinner from** the error of his way will save a **soul from death** and cover a multitude of sins* (James 5:19-20).

James is speaking to fellow Christians, because he refers to them as brothers. The word death in this verse is not talking about physical death, but the death of the soul, "with the implied idea of future misery in hell." A place of "thick darkness" and "wretchedness in hell" (Strong's G5590 / Strong's G2288).

The wonderful thing about the message of James, the prodigal son, and even the lukewarm church, is that there is hope and restoration for all who return to the Lord. No matter how sinful a lifestyle the son was living, he was reinstated to his father's good graces when he turned his back on the sin he was in, and returned home to his father. This promise applies to every person who has ever walked away from the Lord.

What is the Rapture?

We which are alive and remain unto the coming of the Lord shall not prevent (precede) *them which are asleep. For the Lord himself shall descend from heaven with a shout, with the voice of the archangel, and with the trump of God: and the dead in Christ shall rise first: Then we which are alive and remain shall be* **caught up** *together with them in the clouds, to meet the Lord in the air: and so shall we ever be with the Lord* (1 Thessalonians 4:15-17).

This catching away and being changed are called the rapture and the resurrection. The word rapture does not appear in the Bible, but its meaning is there. It is derived from the Latin word *rapturo*, or the Greek word *harpazo*, which means "to seize, to carry off by force, to snatch out or away" (Strong's G726).

The resurrection also happens at this time. This is when believers are changed and given perfect immortal bodies like the one Jesus received when he rose from the dead.

The Bible says, *Behold, I shew you a mystery; We shall not all sleep* (die)*, but we shall all be changed, In a moment, in the twinkling of an eye, at the last trump: for the* *trumpet shall sound, and the dead shall be raised incorruptible, and we shall be changed* (1 Corinthians 15:51-52).

This supernatural event takes place for those in Christ at the time of His return, after the dead are resurrected and meet Him in the air.

Jesus confirmed this time frame when He said, *"This is the will of Him who sent Me, that everyone who sees the Son and believes in Him may have everlasting life; and **I will raise him up at the last day**"* (John 6:40, 44, 54).

In one moment, in the twinkling of an eye, yes, quicker than you can blink an eye, everything will change!

There are three main camps concerning when the rapture will take place that all center around the seven year tribulation period. They are pre-Tribulation, mid-Tribulation, and post-Tribulation. All three views have valid points, but the important thing to remember is that no matter which time-frame is true, we should ALWAYS be ready for this event.

As mentioned earlier, Ruth Graham once said, "I would rather prepare myself to go through the tribulation and be happily surprised by an unexpected rapture, than expect to be raptured only to find myself going through the tribulation."

Jesus told the disciples that no one knows the day or the hour, but that we would see the signs and know that the time is near.

*Now learn this parable from the fig tree: When its branch has already become tender and puts forth leaves, **you know that summer is near**. So you also, **when you see all these things, know that it is near—at the doors!** Assuredly, I* *say to you, this generation will by no means pass away till all these things take place* (Matthew 24:32-34).

Seasonal transitions are easy to recognize. When leaves change from green to red and yellow, we may not know the *day or hour* the leaves will fall from the tree, but we do know that winter will soon follow.

The following are the three major stances as to when the rapture will take place.

The pre-Tribulation belief is primarily based on God's actions in the past. When God caused the great flood during the time of Noah, and the destruction of Sodom and Gomorrah during the time of Lot, and the destruction of Jericho during the time of Rahab, a small group of believers were set apart before the judgment and destruction occurred.

Another reason why many hold to the pre-trib position is because there is no mention of the church after Revelation chapter four when the time of testing begins. This is also where the apostle John sees *a door* opened in heaven, he hears a voice that sounds like a trumpet, and he is called up and immediately finds himself in the throne room of heaven.

Many Christians also believe that the marriage supper of the Lamb will take place during the Tribulation period. This idea follows the tradition of the ancient Jewish wedding celebrations that lasted seven days, or in the case of the Tribulation, seven years.

This future seven day (seven year) celebration and feast theory is not scripturally accurate though, because the Bible states that the marriage supper of the Lamb will take place when Jesus returns with his bride at the *end* of the Tribulation (Revelation 19:7-9).

Another belief is that because God shut the door for Noah and his family when they were safely inside the ark, seven days before the flood came, He will do the same before the Tribulation begins (Genesis 7:10).

Pre-tribulation believers also use the aforementioned verses in 1 Corinthians 15:51-52 and 1 Thessalonians 4:15-17, to support their stance.

The mid-Tribulation camp holds to the scripture that says, *God has not appointed his people to wrath.* Therefore, some people believe that Christians will be raptured before the final 3 ½ years years begin.

This is partly because they are looking at Revelation chapter 11 where it speaks of God's wrath, but this section is actually an overview of the last 3 ½ years of the Tribulation. The chapter begins with the witnesses and then moves onto their martyrdom, and then wraps up with the rapture and day of Judgment (Revelation 11:12, 18).

One of the verses used to support the mid-tribulation stance is [they declare] *how you turned to God from idols to serve the living and true God, and to wait for His Son from heaven, whom He raised from the dead, even **Jesus who delivers us from the wrath to come*** (1 Thessalonians 1:10).

Paul also states in another place that *God did not appoint us to **wrath**, but to obtain salvation through our Lord Jesus Christ* (1 Thessalonians 5:9). These verses are referring to being delivered from the wrath that comes from lack of salvation. It is the same word Paul used in Romans

5:9. *Much more then, having now been justified by His blood, we shall be saved from **wrath** through Him.*

This is also the same word found in John 3:36. *He who believes in the Son has everlasting life; and he who does not believe the Son shall not see life, but the **wrath** of God abides on him.*

All of the above verses have to do with wrath that befalls those outside of Christ, who reject, refuse, or ignore His gift of grace and love (orgē - Strong's G3709).

Even if this was referring to events in Revelation, the wrath of God does not take place until the end of the seven years when Christ returns as Judge and King.

Other supporting verses concerning His wrath **when He returns** are found in Revelation 14:19; 16:19; 19:15. Not that any wrath is tolerable, but the previous wrath is not the same word interpretation or intensity as the wrath verses found at the end of the Tribulation, right before Jesus returns (thymos - G2372).

This becomes more clear when we understand the structure of Revelation, which I explain in the next chapter.

There is also often confusion between God's wrath and human persecution. Since the early days and years of Christianity, to the present time, Christians have been periodically persecuted, tortured and slain. This is not God's wrath, but rather humanity's evil treatment of other human beings, which will continue to escalate until Christ returns.

Satan's wrath is also part of this messy mix. We know this because a voice from heaven proclaims, *Woe to the inhabitants of the earth and the sea! For the devil has come down to you, having great **wrath**, because he knows that he has a short time* (Revelation 12:12).

The post-tribulation group believes that the rapture will happen after the Tribulation when Christ returns as King, to conquer evil at the battle of Armageddon. *Jesus said, Immediately after the tribulation of those days...they shall see the Son of man coming in the clouds of heaven with power and great glory. And he shall send his angels with a great sound of a trumpet, and they shall gather together his elect* (Christians or chosen ones - Strong's G1588) *from the four winds, from one end of heaven to the other* (Matthew 24:29-31).

One of the main verses post-tribulation believers use as proof is the last bowl judgment in Revelation.

All of the leaders [and their armies] *of the earth and of the whole world, gather* [for] *the battle of that great day of God Almighty.* Then Jesus says, *"**Behold, I am coming as a thief.**" And they gathered them together to the place called in Hebrew, **Armageddon*** (Revelation 16:14-16).

They also reference the Bible verse that says the resurrection happens at the rapture when Christ returns. *For in Christ all shall be made alive. But each one in his own order: Christ the firstfruits, **afterward those who are Christ's at His coming. Then comes the end*** (1 Corinthians 15:22-24).

Understanding the Structure of Revelation

The End Times are divided into three main time-frames that follow one another. Although there are many prophecies that have to do with future events in the Old Testament and the epistles, most of the supporting scriptures concerning the Tribulation period and the Second Coming are found in Matthew 24-25 and the book of Revelation.

The Beginning of Sorrows or "birth pangs" (KJV). Jesus said that once these events begin to take place that things will move quickly and anguish will follow. They will be like a woman in labor whose contractions grow in intensity and frequency the closer she is to giving birth. This pain and suffering takes place during the first 3 ½ years of the seven year tribulation period.

As [Jesus] *sat upon the mount of Olives, the disciples came unto him privately, saying, Tell us, when shall these things be? and what shall be the sign of thy coming, and of the end of the world?*

And Jesus answered and said unto them, Take heed that no man deceive you. For many shall come in my name, saying, **I am Christ; and shall deceive many**. *And you will hear of wars and rumors of wars. See that you are not* *troubled; for all these things must come to pass, but the end is not yet. For **nation will rise against nation, and kingdom against kingdom**. And there will be famines, pestilences, and earthquakes in various places. All these are the **beginning of sorrows.*** *Then **they will deliver you up to tribulation and kill you,** and you will be hated by all nations for My name's sake* (Matthew 24:6-8).

These same sorrows are also found in the first four seals of Revelation 6:2-8.

- The first seal is the white horse and its rider is the Antichrist (the deceiver and a possible pandemic).

- The second seal is the red horse and its rider takes peace from the earth (nation will rise against nation and kingdom against kingdom).

- The third seal is the black horse and its rider incites widespread famine (there will be famines and pandemics).

- The fourth seal is the pale horse and its rider is death and martyrdom (they will deliver you up to tribulation and kill you).

The **Great Tribulation** follows the *beginning of sorrows* and takes place during the latter 3 ½ years. This is when the Antichrist and false prophet begin their reign of terror. This is when the Mark of the Beast is enforced and persecution abounds. This is when death, destruction, and devastation are everywhere (Revelation 11, 12, 13).

77

The devastation in Matthew 24:15-21 coincides with the fourth and fifth seals of Revelation, which is martyrdom (that began when the fourth seal was opened): *When He opened the fifth seal, I saw under the altar the souls of those who had been slain for the word of God and for the testimony which they held* (Revelation 6:9).

The Day of the Lord (or **that Day**) is a term used to describe the physical return of Jesus Christ and His triumphant conquest over evil at the battle of Armageddon. These and other verses were mentioned earlier and also confirm this event.

- *But of **that day** and hour no one knows, not even the angels of heaven, but My Father only* (Matthew 24:36).

- *Take heed to yourselves, lest your hearts be weighed down with carousing, drunkenness, and cares of this life, and **that Day** come on you unexpectedly* (Luke 21:34).

- *The sun shall be turned into darkness, and the moon into blood, before the coming of the great and awesome **day of the Lord*** (Acts 2:20).

- *For you yourselves know perfectly that **the day of the Lord** so comes as a thief in the night* (1 Thessalonians 5:2).

The book of Revelation was written by the Apostle John. This is the same John who walked with Jesus on the earth for over three years. Of the twelve disciples, he was one of the three who were closest to Jesus. He is also the same apostle who wrote the books of *John,* and *1, 2, 3 John* in the New Testament.

John was exiled to the Isle of Patmos, which is off the southwest coast of Turkey, for being a Christian and preaching the gospel of Jesus, while under the tyrannical reign of Emperor Domitian. According to Tertullian, an early Christian theologian, prior to John's exile, he had been plunged into boiling oil in Rome and miraculously emerged unhurt.

While in Patmos (around 95 A.D.), John received a vision from Jesus Christ and wrote down everything he saw and heard. The first chapter of Revelation opens by telling us the purpose of this book, which is the unveiling of future events by Jesus Christ, so that we will know what to expect at that time.

The Revelation of Jesus Christ, which God gave Him to show His servants—things which must shortly take place.

There is also a promise of blessing to those who read and heed the warnings. *Blessed is he who reads and those who hear the words of this prophecy, and keep those things which are written in it; for the time is near* (Revelation 1:1, 3).

Next, we see an introduction to who Jesus is, the purpose of His first coming, and the promise of His Second Coming.

He is the faithful witness to these things, the first to rise from the dead, and the ruler of all the kings of the world. [Jesus] ***loves us and has freed us from our sins by shedding his blood for us****. He is the one who comes with the clouds of heaven* (Revelation 1:5, 7 NLT).

Then Jesus declares, *"I am the Alpha and the Omega—the beginning and the end. I am the one who is, who always was, and who is still to come—the Almighty One"* (v.8).

It is important to know that Revelation is not entirely in chronological order. Once this is understood, it clears up many misunderstandings. For example, Revelation chapter one mentions Christ returning in the clouds (v. 7). This brief mention of the Second Coming doesn't take place until the end of the seven year Tribulation, so this first chapter seems to serve as an introduction.

Another key to understanding Revelation is knowing that some events are happening at the same time. For example, in chapters 11, 12 and 13, we see three different scenes where martyrdom is taking place. **The common denominator in these three chapters is that they are all happening during the same 3 ½ year time-frame, so we know that this is true**.

In these three chapters, one scene is viewed from an earthly perspective. Another is viewed from the heavenly realm. And yet another from the spiritual plane close to earth where principalities, powers, rulers of the darkness of this world and spiritual wickedness reside (Ephesians 6:12). Therefore, these three different perspectives are all taking place during the same 3 ½ year time-frame.

This seemingly overlapping of events can be compared to news reports in three different cities that show video footage of protests and riots happening at the same time. If a person penned these three separate views in a book (instead of streaming them on a screen), it would appear to be unfolding chronologically over time, when in reality the events all happened on the same day.

Therefore, the 3 ½ year time stamp confirms that the events are happening concurrently (Revelation 11:3; 12:6; 13:5).

The future events prophesied in Revelation (and Daniel) are also shown as sidebars, overviews, wide-angle views, and close-up views. Another way to think of this method of writing is by looking at a calendar. Some calendars show us the entire year at a glance. On others we see the whole month, and still others we see a week, or even a single day with an hour by hour schedule.

The events in Revelation are often arranged this way. Therefore, if needed, I will explain the perspective when we get to those places.

The Seven Churches of Revelation

Details concerning the seven churches of Revelation are found in chapters 1-3. Jesus appears in all His glory to the apostle John while on the island of Patmos. Christ then dictates to John what to write in seven letters, concerning the spiritual state of the seven churches, which are His people or followers, not a building or denomination.

The seven churches are located in seven cities in Asia Minor (Turkey). Even though the letters were written to those specific churches in A.D. 95, it is safe to say that these are also seven TYPES of churches throughout history up to our present day.

This is very possible because basic human nature and behaviors have not changed a great deal throughout the ages. This is why all of Jesus' teachings are applicable to life, no matter what century they are read.

Knowing this, Christians can relate to the original churches' desires, struggles, strengths and weaknesses, as Jesus' praises, rebukes, and tells them how to correct any similar traits or wayward behaviors at any given time.

Again, these seven churches are NOT the Baptist, Methodist, Catholic, Lutheran, Episcopalian, Pentecostal or any other religious group. At the time of John's writing, there were no such denominations.

The *believers themselves are the church* of Jesus Christ, not a building or a group who hold similar views on rules, traditions, bylaws, or man-made doctrines. The church is a body of Christian individuals who use the Bible as the foundation of their faith, to know God's will and to follow Christ.

Jesus calls His church "candlesticks" or "lampstands." These sources of light are similar to the seven branched menorahs that are lit with wicks and burn olive oil. We know these lampstands are the churches, because Jesus immediately says they are: *"The seven lampstands which you saw are the seven churches"* (Revelation 1:20).

The seven churches are Ephesus, Smyrna, Pergamum, Thyatira, Sardis, Philadelphia, and Laodicea. In five of the seven churches, there are Christians who are both faithful and unfaithful, but of the seven churches, only two are deemed worthy of praise with no rebuke: Smyrna and Philadelphia. The other five have serious problems. One has stopped loving Christ. The others have become liberal, corrupt, unresponsive, worldly, or apathetic.

Yet in His reprimand, Jesus gives them all a chance to repent and do his will, so they may receive a reward, position, and place in His kingdom.

Immediately after John receives these messages, he sees an open door in heaven: *After these things I looked, and behold, a door standing open in heaven. And the first voice which I heard was like a trumpet speaking with me, saying, "Come up here, and I will show you things which must take place after this." Immediately I was in the Spirit; and behold, a throne set in heaven, and One sat on the throne* (Revelation 4:1-2).

We see a connection with the door again. Jesus said, *I am the door: by Me if any man enter in, he shall be saved* (John 10:9). Jesus is the door and He is the way into the throne room of God where John is about to get a panoramic view of the Almighty God and the future of mankind. John sees the beauty of heaven, along with the elders and angelic beings who are praising and worshiping God in all His glory.

[Those in the throne room] *sang a new song, saying: "You are worthy to take the scroll, and to open its seals; for You were slain, and have redeemed us to God by Your blood out of every tribe and tongue and people and nation* (Revelation 5:9).

And then the Lamb, Jesus, is given a scroll that has been kept closed with seven wax seals. When the first seal is opened, the Tribulation begins (Revelation 6).

What is the Tribulation Period?

The Tribulation is a seven year period of God's testing and discipline to bring people to repentance, and to judge those who refuse to repent and receive His gift of forgiveness and eternal life. This is the *great time of testing that will come upon the whole world to test those who belong to this world* (Revelation 3:10b).

Before Revelation was ever written, the Old Testament prophet Daniel had similar visions of the Last Days. He also said concerning this time that, *"Many will be purified, cleansed, and refined by these trials"* (12:10).

Daniel prophesied many events that will take place during the final 3 ½ years before Christ returns. He also prophesied that during that time *many will rush here and there and knowledge will increase* (Daniel 12:4 NLT).

Daniel saw that fast transportation and the explosion of information would be two signs of the end times, and they are here. The ease at which data can be transmitted and received has grown exponentially since the 1980s with the use of computers and the World Wide Web. We carry a device in the palm of our hand that can transmit huge amounts of information within seconds, to another device thousands of miles away. The cell phones, laptops, and tablets that we now take for granted were unheard of before the mid-1970s (PCs) and 80s (Internet).

The other modern marvel is the speed at which we can travel. In the past 100 years we have gone from horses, trains, boats, and bikes as modes of transportation, to high-speed cars, trans-Atlantic planes, sound barrier breaking jets, and rockets to the moon.

Many rush from here-to-there and knowledge has increased, in a matter of decades just as Daniel prophesied.

As amazing as these prophecies were at that time, Daniel's most profound visions foretold the coming of the Messiah: His first physical appearance on earth, His death, and events leading up to His return and His eternal kingdom.

Bible scholars refer to this as "The seventy weeks of Daniel." These weeks actually represent years. Sixty-nine of those "weeks" were fulfilled in the years leading up to the first coming of Christ. After His death there is a gap of at least 2,000 years between the 69th and the 70th week, because He was "cut off" (died) as prophesied (Daniel 9:24-26).

The seventieth week (of seven years) is yet to come.

During the middle of the Tribulation (the second 3½ years), the Abomination of Desolation is set up and the Mark of the Beast is enforced. This is the starting point for The *Great* Tribulation, or the Time of Jacob's (Israel) Trouble. This time is also referred to as 42 months or 1,260 days in the books of Daniel (12:7b) and Revelation chapters 11, 12 and 13. This means that these chaotic events and the mass persecution (mentioned in these three chapters) will be happening **at the same time** in Israel and around the world.

- The Gentiles *will tread the holy city* (Jerusalem) *underfoot for* **forty-two months** (3 ½ years). The beast (the government empowered by Satan) will war against those who don't conform to their decrees, and eventually kill them (Revelation 11:3, 7).

- When Satan is thrown from the heavenly realm, his reign of terror on earth begins. *Now when the dragon* (Satan) *saw that he had been cast to the earth, he persecuted the woman* (Israel) *who gave birth to the male Child* (Jesus). *But the woman was given two wings of a great eagle, that she might fly into the wilderness to her place, where she is nourished for* **a time and times and half a time** (3 ½ years), *from the presence of the serpent* (Revelation 12:13-14).

- The Last Days leader (Antichrist) will rule the global government for 3 ½ years. He will demand strict allegiance to his rules and enforce worldwide persecution to those who don't comply by honoring him as God and savior of the world.

[The Antichrist] *was given a mouth speaking great things and blasphemies, and he was given authority to continue for* **forty-two months (3 ½ years)**. *Then he opened his mouth in blasphemy against God, to blaspheme His name, His tabernacle, and those who dwell in heaven. It was granted to him to make war with the saints and to overcome them* (Revelation 13:5-7).

- Daniel also mentions the 3 ½ years of persecution.

[The persecution] *shall be for **a time, times, and half a time**; and when the power of the holy people has been completely shattered, all these things shall be finished. "Go your way, Daniel, for the words are closed up and sealed till the time of the end"* (Daniel 12:7b, 9).

The following verse in Revelation is in reference to the above prophecy of Daniel. *In the days of the sounding of the **seventh angel, when he is about to sound, the mystery of God would be finished**, as He declared to His servants the prophets* (Revelation 10:7).

The fulfillment of the **mystery of God** is the seventh angel sounding **the last trumpet** prior to the rapture and resurrection when Christ's returns. *Behold, I tell you a mystery: We shall not all sleep* (die), *but we shall all be changed—in a moment, in the twinkling of an eye, at the **last trumpet**. For **the trumpet will sound, and the dead will be raised incorruptible, and we shall be changed*** (1 Corinthians 15:51-52).

The seven year Tribulation ends at the battle of Armageddon. Then, the Millennial reign of Jesus Christ, the eternal King of everyone and everything begins.

Examples of Possible Symbols and Meanings

The apostle John saw many wild-sights and catastrophes that he did not fully understand. When we consider the fact that he was looking into the future and seeing our world today, with all of its inventions and technology, everything would have looked miraculous or monstrous to him. Therefore, John described what he saw by comparing it to what he knew.

If we compare John's prophecies to a person living 500 years ago, who had a vision of a vacuum cleaner, the person may have said something like this: "I saw a beast shaped like a barrel but it moved on wheels. It had a trunk like an elephant, but it roared like a lion. And as the trunk was pushed along the floor, it devoured dust and debris in its path."

We would know that the person was describing the canister and hose of a vacuum cleaner, along with the noise of the motor and the suction feature. But since John had no clue about modern marvels that we have now, he described what he saw using things that he was familiar with during his lifetime.

Many of John's visions refer to the spiritual realm, but some pertain to the physical world. A few present day inventions and events make some of his mysteries easier to decode. For example, the prophecy concerning the martyrdom of Christians says, *"Then those from the peoples, tribes, tongues, and nations will see their dead bodies three-and-a-half days* (Revelation 11:9).

This event is obviously being seen all over the world, which was impossible during John's lifetime, but it is possible today with satellites beaming live stream news to media sources all over the globe.

Prophecy is often like deciphering a code. John even uses the word "like" approximately twenty to thirty-eight times (depending on the Bible version) in many of his descriptions, because he did not fully understand what he was seeing, so he used comparisons.

The following are just a few examples of possible interpretations, to give an idea of what they may mean. I am not saying these are right or wrong. Just possibilities. Throughout the remainder of this book I will clarify when something is my interpretation by saying things such as, "It is possible," or "This may be," or "this could be," or other similar remarks.

Blood, Fire and Pillars of Smoke or Bombs?

God said (in the last days), *"I will pour out My Spirit on all flesh. And I will show wonders in the heavens and in the earth: **Blood and fire and pillars of smoke**. The sun shall be turned into darkness, and the moon into blood, before the coming of the great and awesome day of the Lord. And it shall come to pass that whoever calls on the name of the Lord shall be saved"* (Joel 2:28a, 30-32). This prophecy concerning the Day of the Lord is repeated in Acts 2:17-21; Matthew 24:29 and Revelation 6:12.

How can smoke be controlled to look like columns? Volcanic eruptions, oil well fires, bombs? All of these are possibilities. When Saddam Hussein set the oil wells in Kuwait and Iraq on fire, we saw (on television via satellite) hundreds of pillars of smoke from the oil that burned for months. This caused so much environmental damage that the smoke darkened the sun for days.

An atomic bomb also appears like a pillar of smoke as it rises and forms a mushroom cloud upon impact.

We also understand through this prophetic imagery that the moon does not literally turn to blood, but that some external agent causes it to appear red such as smoke from forest fires. We also now know through organizations like NASA that the moon goes through intermittent cycles of "turning red" or what we now call blood moons, which are caused by light shining at different angles during a lunar eclipse.

The Bottomless Pit or CERN?

*Then the fifth angel blew his trumpet, and I saw **a star that had fallen to earth from the sky, and he was given the key to the shaft of the bottomless pit**. When he opened it, smoke poured out as though from a huge furnace, and the sunlight and air turned dark from the smoke. Their king is the angel from the bottomless pit; his name in Hebrew is Abaddon, and in Greek, **Apollyon—the Destroyer*** (Revelation 9:1, 2, 11).

This is most likely Satan and his demonic minions, because they have already been cast down to the earthly realm from the heavenly realm (Revelation 12:9-13). Satan is the prince of the power of the air, and he moves about like a roaring lion amid our earthly domain, seeking whom he may devour (Ephesians 2:2; 1 Peter 5:8).

This may also have something to do with CERN (Conseil Européen pour la Recherche Nucléaire), the European Organization for Nuclear Research that is located near Geneva, Switzerland.

CERN is an underground facility that is 575 feet deep with a seventeen mile tunnel system, and its logo is the intertwining of the number 666 (which is the number of the Beast). A statue of the Hindu god Lord Shiva, whose name means the "Destroyer of the Universe," stands outside CERN's headquarters. This may or may not have anything to do with the prophecy in Revelation, but it is a noteworthy "coincidence."

Locusts or Helicopters?

Then locusts came from the smoke and descended on the earth, and they were given power to sting like scorpions. **They were told not to harm the grass or plants or trees, but only the people who did not have the seal of God** *on their foreheads.*

The locusts looked like horses prepared for battle. They had what looked like gold crowns on their heads, and their faces looked like human faces. They had hair like women's hair and teeth like the teeth of a lion. They wore armor made of iron, and their wings roared like an army of chariots rushing into battle. They had tails that stung like scorpions, and for five months they had the power to torment people (Revelation 9:3, 4, 7-10).

The locusts described here are not flying insects. We know this because locusts can devour acres of vegetation in a very short time, yet these "locusts" do not harm the grass, plants, trees or Christians, but only the people *who do not belong to God.*

Locusts also do not attack, bite, or sting humans, nor do they carry diseases that harm them, yet these locusts sting like scorpions and cause pain that lasts up to five months.

So what could this be? It sounds like the description of a military helicopter. These "locusts" look like horses prepared for battle. They have breastplates of "iron" (the body of the helicopter). They have a crown (propeller), the face of a human (the pilot) and they sting with their tails like a scorpion (auto-cannons, guns, and ammo). They also sound like chariots rushing to battle (engines roaring and propellers whirring).

These may or may not be military helicopters, but they certainly are not locusts as we know them. They also could be combat drones.

Chariots or Cars?

In John's vision of the destruction of Babylon, he saw all types of merchandise and livestock and chariots, among other things, being destroyed (Revelation 18:10-13). This particular word, chariot, is found only once in the Bible, and it is translated as *a type of vehicle having **four** wheels* (Strong's G4480).

John did not use the typical word to describe a two-wheeled chariot pulled by horses that he would have recognized from his time. This may mean that he was seeing cars or trucks amid the devastation. And since he did not know what they were, the closest things he could compare them to were four wheeled chariots.

What are the Seven Seals?

The seals in Revelation chapter six are referring to wax seals that keep scrolls closed. The seven seals are an overview or "Table of Contents" of the tribulation period and the Second Coming of Christ. The seals also follow the timeline in Jesus' Olivet Discourse concerning these same end-time events (Matthew 24:2-31).

The Lamb, Jesus, opens the first seal to reveal the first of four horsemen.

THE FIRST SEAL is a white horse and its rider is the Antichrist. *I looked up and saw a white horse standing there. Its rider carried a bow, and a crown was placed on his head. He rode out to win many battles and gain the victory* (Revelation 6:2).

The rider wears a crown and carries a bow, but no arrows. He arrives on the scene as a powerful leader who conquers by peace, most likely through promises of prosperity and land negotiations. He will use subtle means to entice the masses with things that appear to benefit humanity, but these things will quickly lead them into bondage while under his control.

The rider on this white horse has the appearance of a savior, but the true Savior returns seven years later on a white horse, as King of kings and Lord of lords. His weapon is a fiery sword that comes out of His mouth, which means He slays His enemies with the Words that He speaks (Ephesians 6:17; Hebrews 4:12; Revelation 19:12).

The rider on the white horse is the impostor who poses as the savior. He is the Antichrist who comes in peace, but changes his behavior and becomes a dictator who demands to be worshiped as god.

He wears a crown, but it is not a royal crown. It is a laurel wreath which was given to winners in public (Olympic) games (Strong's G4735). This perishable crown is a glaring contrast to the many royal crowns (diadems) that Jesus wears when He returns as king and rides in triumph to fight at the battle of Armageddon (Strong's G1238; Revelation 19:12).

The prophet Daniel also wrote about the Antichrist when he said, *"He shall magnify himself in his heart, and by peace shall destroy many* (Daniel 8:25 KJV).

This leader will attempt to take the place of Christ and will not tolerate anyone who competes for his devotion, honor, or obedience. The Antichrist's decrees will affect the true followers of Christ the most, because he will attempt to rid the world of their presence.

The first seal parallel in Matthew 24:5. *Many will come in My name, saying, 'I am the Christ,' and will deceive many.*

There may also be a concurrent event to consider when the First Seal is opened. If we examine the bow and the crown, there is a startling correlation between these symbols of power and events that have happened (or may happen in the future).

The First Seal says, *I looked, and behold, a white horse. He who sat on it had a **bow**; and a **crown** was given to him, and he went out **conquering and to conquer*** (Revelation 6:2).

If we analyze this section again, the word bow in the original Greek means *toxon*, which is where we get the word toxic (Strongs G5115). (This is the only place in the Bible where the word "bow" is used in this unique form.) It is also important to note that this toxin is not referring to poisonous arrows, because there are no arrows. The toxic substance is being released from the bow the leader is holding and controlling. Therefore, the rider on the white horse is conquering with a weapon that unleashes something toxic *that we cannot see.*

It is also interesting to note that the one causing the devastation wears a crown. And the Latin word for crown is "corona." These sidenotes may or may not be of any significance, but they are something to think about.

THE SECOND SEAL is a red horse and its rider takes peace from the earth. The rider is *given a mighty sword and the authority to take peace from the earth. And there was war and slaughter everywhere* (Revelation 6:4 NLT). This verse is self-explanatory, as there will be conflict, chaos, and wars all over the world. This mighty sword may not be an actual sword, because John did not always understand what he was seeing. These may be large caliber guns or other heavy artillery used as weapons of war.

The second seal parallel in Matthew 24:7. *Nation will rise against nation, and kingdom against kingdom* (Matthew 24:7).

THE THIRD SEAL is a black horse and its rider creates widespread famine. The rider holds a pair of scales in his hand, which are used for weighing food, but here they are used to symbolize famine. This may be a result of wildfires, wars or drought, which leads to scarcity or hyperinflation.

An example of how this may unfold is by looking at what happened in Ukraine and Russia. Both countries supply approximately 30% of the world's wheat and 30% of the world's barley. Russia also supplies massive amounts of fertilizer to countries around the world. A lack of these crucial exports will create grain shortages and lower future crop yields, which would then inflate the cost of food. This type of crisis or one similar to it may be how the third seal of Revelation eventually unfolds.

I looked up and saw a black horse, and its rider was holding a pair of scales in his hand. And I heard a voice from among the four living beings say, "A loaf of wheat bread or three loaves of barley will cost a day's pay" (Revelation 6:5-6).

A lack of food and nutrients also lowers a person's resistance to infectious diseases. This may contribute to the further spread of the pandemics (pestilences) that Jesus said would occur.

The third seal parallel in Matthew 24:7-8. *There will be famines, pestilences, and earthquakes in various places. All these are the beginning of sorrows.*

THE FOURTH SEAL is a pale horse and its rider is death and the grave follows. These have the power to kill over one-fourth of the people on earth with the *sword, famine, disease and wild animals* (Revelation 6:8).

The sword here may be referring to beheading, because it will be the primary method of execution for those who stand for Christ and refuse the Mark of the Beast.

I saw the souls of those who had been beheaded for their witness to Jesus and for the word of God, who had not worshiped the beast or his image, and had not received his mark on their foreheads or on their hands (Revelation 20:4).

The famine, disease, and animal attacks may be the result of people living off the grid and unable to buy food when the Mark is enforced. Inadequate shelter exposes people to the elements. Poor nutrition, due to lack of food, makes them vulnerable to disease. Living off the grid leaves them open to animal attacks. These are possible results from not having enough food to survive.

The fourth seal (above) and fifth seal (below) describe martyrdom, which takes place in the middle of the tribulation (3 ½ years into the seven years).

THE FIFTH SEAL brings more death. We know this because we see the martyrs' *souls* in heaven, and they are told that *more Christians will be slain and join them.*

Since it is their *souls* that cry out, we know that they have not been physically resurrected yet. This means that these people in heaven are not raptured believers. We know this because when the dead and the living are raptured, they will be instantly changed and given immortal bodies (1 Corinthians 15:51-53).

*When He opened the fifth seal, I saw under the altar the **souls of those who had been slain** for the word of God and for the testimony which they held. And they cried with a loud voice, saying, "How long, O Lord, holy and true, until You judge and avenge our blood on those who dwell on the earth?" Then a white robe was given to each of them; and it was said to them that they should rest a little while longer, **until both the number of their fellow servants and their brethren, who would be killed as they were, was completed*** (Revelation 6:9-11).

The fourth and fifth seal parallel in Matthew 24:9-12 is martyrdom. *"Then they will deliver you up to tribulation and kill you, and **you will be hated by all nations for My name's sake**. And then many will be offended, will betray one another, and will hate one another. Then many false prophets will rise up and deceive many. And because lawlessness* (sin) *will abound, the love of many will grow cold."*

Details of this mass persecution and slaughter in the fourth and fifth seals are not mentioned until Revelation chapters 11, 12, and 13, concerning those who hold firm to Jesus and the Word of God. Therefore, these events are happening during the final 3 ½ years. We know this because there is no evidence of Christian persecution under the Antichrist's rule before chapter 11 when the two witnesses come on the scene.

Thus, the fourth and fifth seals take place in the middle of the tribulation and continue on until Christ returns 3 ½ years later in the sixth seal. This is the beginning of the Great Tribulation, persecution and mass martyrdom.

THE SIXTH SEAL brings catastrophes and events that are prophesied to happen at the Second Coming of Christ. When we compare the specific events in Revelation 6:12-17 with Matthew 24 and Old Testament prophecies, it is clear that these passages are all describing the same events surrounding the return of Jesus.

*I looked when He opened the **sixth seal**, and behold, there was a **great earthquake**; and the **sun became black** as sackcloth of hair, and **the moon became like blood**. And **the stars of heaven fell to the earth**, as a fig tree drops its late figs when it is **shaken** by a mighty wind. Then the sky receded as a scroll when it is rolled up, and **every mountain and island was moved out of its place**. And the kings of the earth, the great men, the rich men, the commanders, the mighty men, every slave and every free man, **hid themselves** in the caves and in the rocks of the mountains, and said to the mountains and rocks, "**Fall on us and hide us from the face of Him who sits on the throne and from the wrath of the Lamb! For the great day of His wrath has** come, and who is able to stand?"* (Revelation 6:12-17).

The sixth seal parallel in Matthew 24:29-31. *Immediately after the tribulation of those days **the sun will be darkened, and the moon will not give its light; the stars will fall from heaven**, and the powers of the heavens will be **shaken**. Then the sign of the **Son of Man will appear in heaven**, and then **all the tribes of the earth will mourn**, and they will see **the Son of Man coming on the clouds of heaven** with power* *and great glory. And He will send His angels with a great* **sound of a trumpet, and they will gather together His elect** *from the four winds, from one end of heaven to the other.*

The word "elect" in Matthew 24:31 is interpreted by Strong's Lexicon as Christians, not solely the Jewish people (Strong's G1588 - 1. Chosen by God to obtain salvation through Christ. 2. Christians are called "chosen or elect" of God).

THE SEVENTH SEAL opens with silence in heaven. When Jesus returns, this silence may indicate that the heavenly court is in session.

The seventh seal parallel in Matthew 25:1-46 also describes what happens when Christ returns. Here we see three groups of people (the virgins, the servants, and the sheep and the goats) who all appear to be Christians, but there is a separation going on within each group. (More on this later.)

We also see another view of a courtroom scene in Revelation chapter 11, when Christ returns and begins to rule and reign.

Then the seventh angel sounded: And there were loud voices in heaven, saying, "The kingdoms of this world have become the kingdoms of our Lord and of His Christ, and He shall reign forever and ever! The nations were angry, and **Your wrath has come, and the time of the dead, that they should be judged,** *and that You should reward Your servants the prophets and the saints, and those who fear Your name, small and great, and should destroy those who destroy the earth"* (Revelation 11:15, 18).

Who are the 144,000 and the Souls in Heaven?

There is a gap between the sixth and seventh seals where we see another scene with two groups of people. Revelation chapter seven seems to be a sidebar or snapshot of what is to come. It is a very quick view of the Jewish converts and a vast multitude of martyred Christians in heaven (Revelation 7:4, 9).

The 144,000 receive a seal from God on their foreheads, which indicates that they have received the Holy Spirit (Revelation 7:4-8). This seal of the spirit is always given to those who receive Christ as Savior. The Bible says, *In Him* (Jesus) *you also trusted, after you heard the word of truth, the gospel of your salvation; in whom also, having believed,* **you were sealed with the Holy Spirit** *of promise* (Ephesians 1:13).

This promise is also confirmed in 2 Corinthians: *He who establishes us with you in Christ and has anointed us is God, who also has* **sealed us and given us the Spirit** *in our hearts as a guarantee* (1:21-22).

We do not hear anything more about the 144,000 again until chapter 14, when they are in heaven with Jesus before He returns.

The next scene is a glimpse of a multitude of people from every nation, tribe, and language praising God in heaven.

After these things I looked, and behold, a great multitude (of people) *which no one could number, of all nations, tribes, peoples, and tongues, **standing** before the throne and before the Lamb, clothed with white robes, with palm branches in their **hands**, and crying out with a loud voice, saying, "Salvation belongs to our God who sits on the throne, and to the Lamb!"* (Revelation 7:9-10).

These people are *standing* and *holding* palm branches in their *hands*, which means they are not *souls*, like we previously saw in the case of the martyrs when they were under the altar in the fifth seal (Revelation 6:9, 11). These believers have resurrected bodies. We know this because a soul does not have the ability to stand or hold onto things.

The Apostle John clarifies by saying that these are the Christians who came out *of* the great tribulation.

Then one of the elders answered, saying to me, "Who are these arrayed in white robes, and where did they come from?" And I said to him, "Sir, you know."

So he said to me, "These are the ones who come out of the great tribulation, and washed their robes and made them white in the blood of the Lamb" (Revelation 7:13-14).

This passage is most likely referring to events happening after the sixth seal when Jesus returned. Therefore, these are the ones who were raptured and resurrected at that time.

The multitudes in heaven are Christians from all over the world who came out of the great tribulation. They are also given the assurance that they will never hunger, thirst or feel the heat of the sun, because Jesus will feed them and lead them to living water. And God wipes away their tears (Revelation 7:9, 14-17).

They shall neither hunger anymore nor thirst anymore; the sun shall not strike them, nor any heat (7:16).

It is obvious that if these people are promised that they will never suffer from thirst, hunger, or intense heat anymore, they must have suffered under these conditions during the Tribulation.

This passage also must be speaking of the time after Christ returns, because Christians cannot have new physical bodies in heaven at the beginning or middle of the Tribulation, because the resurrection does not take place until Christ returns for the battle of Armageddon (Revelation 16:15-16).

*For as in Adam all die, even so in Christ all **shall be made alive**. But each one in his own order: **Christ the firstfruits, afterward those who are Christ's at His coming.** Then comes the end,** when He delivers the kingdom to God the Father, when He puts an end to all rule and all authority and power* (1 Corinthians 15:22-24).

The Seven Trumpets and the Seven Bowls

As mentioned before, one key to reading Revelation is understanding the structure, overviews, sidebars and sequence of events. That being said, it is very possible that the seven trumpet and seven bowl judgments are happening at the same time because they are *very similar* events with a few variations.

A similar example of two visions (dreams) meaning the same thing are found in Genesis when Joseph had two seemingly different prophetic dreams. In one dream Joseph saw twelve sheaves of wheat, which represented him and his brothers. His sheaf rose up and the eleven other sheaves bowed to his sheaf.

In Joseph's second dream, the sun, moon, and eleven stars bowed down to him. This dream contained different elements than the previous one, even though both dreams had the same meaning: Joseph's family would someday bow to him, which they did after he rose to a position of power in Egypt.

Though these dreams seemed like two separate events with a few new details (earthly sheaves compared to the sun, moon and stars), they were really the same event just described in a different way (Genesis 37:5-9).

Pharaoh also had two dreams that Joseph accurately interpreted. The first dream was about two types of cattle. Seven cows were stocky and seven were scrawny. Pharaoh's next dream was about two types of corn. Seven stalks were full and seven were withered. Both dreams symbolized the seven year bounty and the seven year famine that Egypt would experience. Both dreams though seemingly different were one and the same prophetic event (Genesis 41:1-7).

One obvious difference between the trumpet and bowl series of events is that the trumpet judgments are not as intense or widespread as the bowl judgments. The trumpet judgment disasters affect one-third of the earth and people, whereas the Bowl judgments are worse disasters that affect the entire earth and its inhabitants.

What seems to be a disconnect can be justified if we consider that time is causing the disasters to multiply and spread over the course of the 3 ½ years. The *ongoing* devastation becomes worse over time due to the snowball effect. The trumpet judgments seem to evolve into the bowl judgments due to the natural process of deterioration, which creates greater and more widespread devastation. Therefore, the bowl judgments may simply be a culmination of the trumpet judgments that have intensified over time.

The following are descriptions of the trumpet and bowl judgments. Although they are written in sequential order in Revelation there are chapters between them, but they are still similar or ongoing events unfolding and worsening over time. I have put them next to each other to show their similarities and why I believe this is a correct interpretation. I could be totally wrong on this, since no one really knows for sure, but these are possible scenarios.

The first trumpet and bowl judgments do not have obvious similarities, but they may be connected through cause and effect.

FIRST TRUMPET: *The first angel sounded: Hail and fire followed, mingled with blood, and they were thrown to the earth. And a third of the trees were burned up, and all green grass was burned up* (Revelation 8:7).

This may be missile or artillery fire raining down on the earth as a warning, since there is no mention of people being burned or killed.

FIRST BOWL: *The first angel poured out his bowl upon the earth, and a foul and loathsome sore came upon the men* [and women] ***who had the mark of the beast and those who worshiped his image*** (Revelation 16:2).

The description of the sores seem like a severe ulcer that may have an offensive smell. This cannot be the effect of nuclear, chemical, or biological weapons, because the sores are isolated *only to those who received* the Mark of the Beast or who worshiped his image. These sores could be the result of a test run (gone bad) of the Mark before it becomes mandatory. If this is the case, it is possible that the trial version of the Mark becomes infected, or it has other issues that have not been worked out.

The Mark (chip) may also contain a remote controlled agent that can be dispensed electronically. Whoever is in control, may be able to release a pathogen or poison within the chip, or inflict pain on those who rebel against the system. These are all possibilities, because the Mark will be embedded with satellite connecting capabilities, similar to what we have in our smartphones.

SECOND TRUMPET The second angel sounded: *And Something like a great mountain burning with fire was thrown into the sea, and a third of **the sea became blood**. And a third of the living creatures in the sea died, and a third of the ships were destroyed* (Revelation 8:8-9).

This cannot be an actual mountain or volcano, because it has no way to hurl itself into the sea. Volcano lava may flow into the sea, but John would have recognized that if he saw it, and would have said so. This could be a meteor or a nuclear bomb crashing to earth and landing in the sea to poison the water, because it only affects one-third of everything mentioned.

SECOND BOWL: *The second angel poured out his bowl on **the sea, and it became blood** as of a dead man; and every living creature in the sea died* (Revelation 16:3).

This could be an ongoing result of the second trumpet judgment, since both events involve blood in the sea. This may be actual blood or nuclear fallout caused by a bomb releasing radiation into the seas. The second bowl affects the sea just like the second trumpet, but at this point **every** living creature in the sea died.

THIRD TRUMPET: *The third angel sounded: And a great star fell from heaven, burning like a torch, and it fell on a third of the rivers and on the springs of water. The name of the star is Wormwood. **A third of the waters became***

wormwood, and many men died from the water, because it was made bitter (Revelation 8:10-11).

THIRD BOWL: *The third angel poured out his bowl on* **the rivers and springs of water, and they became blood** (Revelation 16:4).

    This could be caused by a meteor or industrial waste runoff, but these are unlikely, since the disaster affects at least one third of the world. Something powerful is contaminating the fresh water and it is quickly spreading. It may be nuclear or biological (warfare) that has naturally or intentionally seeped to the rivers and streams, because the previous judgments (second bowl and second trumpet) both mention the seas turning to blood.

FOURTH TRUMPET: *The fourth angel sounded: And a third of* **the sun** *was struck, a third of the moon, and a third of the stars, so that a third of them were darkened. A third of the day did not shine, and likewise the night* (Revelation 8:12).

    This partial darkness could be caused by smoke, soot, and dust kicked up into the atmosphere from nuclear explosions. These firestorms would partially block the light of the sun, moon, and stars for weeks. All of these toxic emissions could ramp up the greenhouse effect and trap the heat in the atmosphere, which would lead to the fourth bowl judgment of intense heat from the sun.

FOURTH BOWL: *The fourth angel poured out his bowl on* **the sun,** *and power was given to him to scorch men with fire. And men were scorched with great heat, and they blasphemed the name of God who has power over these* *plagues; and **they did not repent and give Him glory*** (Revelation 16:8-9).

Whether global warming is real or not, as many people do and don't believe, God is using a natural disaster (like He did with the flood), to bring people to repentance. Yet sadly, just as in the days of Noah, they will still refuse to repent.

FIFTH TRUMPET: *The fifth angel sounded: And I saw a star fallen from heaven to the earth. To him was given the key to the bottomless pit. And he opened the bottomless pit, and smoke arose out of the pit like the smoke of a great furnace. So **the sun and the air were darkened** because of the smoke of the pit.*

*Then out of the smoke locusts came upon the earth. And to them was given power, as the scorpions of the earth have power. They were commanded not to harm the grass of the earth, or any green thing, or any tree, but **only those men who do not have the seal of God on their foreheads**. And they were not given authority to kill them, but to torment them for five months. **Their torment was like the torment of a scorpion when it strikes a man**. In those days men will seek death and will not find it; they will desire to die, and death will flee from them* (Revelation 9:1-6).

This star that falls from heaven is Satan and / or possibly something from CERN, as mentioned in the chapter "Examples of Possible Symbols and Meanings" (Isaiah 14:12-15; Revelation 12:9). The demonic servants released from this pit may be influencing those who control devices such as helicopters and drones.

At this point, life on earth becomes hell for the unconverted. We know this because these "locusts" are only tormenting non-Christians.

This pain coincides with the fifth bowl judgment.

FIFTH BOWL: *The fifth angel poured out his bowl on the throne of the beast, and **his kingdom became full of darkness;** and **they gnawed their tongues because of the pain*** (Revelation 16:10).

This darkness could be a continuation of the previous judgment (the fourth trumpet) with the sun's partial darkness, or it could be from the smoke that comes out of the bottomless pit, or it could be a smoke plume from a nuclear bomb.

The pain may also be a continuation of the first bowl: *A foul and loathsome sore came upon the men who had the mark of the beast and those who worshiped his image* (Revelation 16:2).

Both the trumpet and bowl judgments refer to the intense pain that those who receive the Mark of the Beast will experience.

SIXTH TRUMPET: The sixth angel sounded *"Release the four **angels who are bound at the great river Euphrates."** So the four angels, who had been prepared for the hour and day and month and year, were released to kill a third of mankind. Now the number of the army of the horsemen was two hundred million; I heard the number of them.*

By these three plagues a third of mankind was killed—by the fire and the smoke and the brimstone which came out of their mouths. For their power is in their mouth and in their tails; for their tails are like serpents, having heads; and with them they do harm (Revelation 9:14-19).

When angels are bound it means they are evil. An army of 200 *million* mounted troops kill one-third of the people by the fire, smoke, and burning sulfur that issues from their horses' mouths.

These may be armed soldiers, missiles, or cannon fire from tanks, since John had never seen modern day artillery. Some people believe this could be Iran or China advancing from the east, because they have enough soldiers to create a 200 million man army. This military advancement will be in place as the world prepares for Aramageddon. This attack will be widespread and cause great devastation in order to kill one-third of humanity.

SIXTH BOWL: *Then the sixth angel poured out his bowl on the great **river Euphrates**, and its water was dried up, so that the way of **the kings from the east** might be prepared. And I saw three unclean spirits like frogs coming out of the mouth of the **dragon**, out of the mouth of the **beast**, and out of the mouth of the **false prophet**. For they are spirits of demons, performing signs, which go out to the kings of the earth and of the whole world, **to gather them to the battle of that great day of God Almighty*** (Revelation 16:12-14).

The Euphrates River dries up and the kings from the east march along the dry riverbed. This drying up of the Euphrates River could be evaporation from the intense heat (due to the scorching sun in the fourth bowl). The river could also be reduced to a trickle by the Atatürk Dam in Turkey.

Then Jesus gives us the warning, the promise, and the purpose of His return: *"Behold, **I am coming as a thief**.*

Blessed is he who watches, and keeps his garments, lest he walk naked and they see his shame." And they gathered them together to the place called in Hebrew, **Armageddon** (Revelation 16:15-16).

When the sixth bowl is poured out the unholy trinity moves into position for the battle of Armageddon. These events set the stage for the final showdown between good and evil when Christ physically returns to earth.

SEVENTH TRUMPET: *Then the seventh angel sounded: And there were* **loud voices in heaven,** *saying,* **"The kingdoms of this world have become the kingdoms of our Lord and of His Christ,** *and He shall reign forever and ever!"*

The nations **were** *angry, and* **Your wrath has come, and the time of the dead, that they should be judged, and that You should reward Your servants** *the prophets and the saints, and those who fear Your name, small and great, and should destroy those who destroy the earth."*

Then the temple of God was opened in heaven, and the ark of His covenant was seen in His temple. And there were **lightnings, noises, thunderings, an earthquake, and great hail** (Revelation 11:15, 18-19).

Notice the key events of Christ's return and subsequent judgment when the Seventh trumpet sounds: Loud voices, lightning and thundering, an earthquake and great hail.

Now notice (below) the same events are happening when the Seventh bowl is poured out: Loud voices, thunderings and lightnings, an earthquake so great that islands disappear and mountains are moved, and huge hailstones fall from the sky.

The seventh bowl is another view of the Second Coming.

SEVENTH BOWL: *Then the seventh angel poured out his bowl into the air, and **a loud voice came out of the temple of heaven**, from the throne, saying, "**It is done!**" And there were **noises and thunderings and lightnings**; and there was **a great earthquake**, such a mighty and great earthquake as had not occurred since men were on the earth. Now the great city was divided into three parts, **and the cities of the nations fell**. And great Babylon was remembered before God, to give her the cup of the wine of the fierceness of His wrath. Then **every island fled away, and the mountains were not found**. And great hail from heaven fell upon men, each hailstone about the weight of a talent* (75 lbs / 34 kg). *Men blasphemed God because of the plague of the hail, since that plague was exceedingly great* (Revelation 16:15-18, 20-21).

The verses above concerning the great earthquake and the islands and mountains being removed are also mentioned in the sixth seal description of events surrounding the Second Coming (Revelation 6:12, 14).

When the seventh bowl is poured out, Jesus returns as conquering king. These are the same events John described in the sixth seal (Revelation 6:12-17) and the seventh (last) trumpet (Revelation 11:15, 18-19), which means they are all the same event.

Who are the Two Witnesses?

Revelation 11, 12 and 13 are happening at the same time during the final 3 ½ years of the Great Tribulation. These three chapters focus on the persecution of Christians and events surrounding that time of terror. We see three different angles and scenes just as we would see in a movie or read in a novel. Some events are an overview, while others are closeup and detailed.

Revelation 11 marks the middle of the seven year tribulation. This chapter is a condensed overview of the last 3 ½ years of the Great Tribulation. The main events mentioned in this chapter are the two witnesses, martyrdom, the rapture, Christ's return to reign, and the final Judgment.

It is here that we are introduced to the two witnesses who prophesy for 3 ½ years and are martyred. The third temple will be in place during this time, and the Temple Mount will be shared by both the Jews and the Gentiles. We know this because the Apostle John tells us so.

The angel stood, saying, "Rise and measure the temple of God, the altar, and those who worship there. But leave out the court which is outside the temple, and do not measure it, for **it has been given to the Gentiles** *(non-Jews). And they will tread the holy city underfoot for* **forty-two months** *(3 ½ years). And I will give power to my two* *witnesses, and they will prophesy 1,260 days* (3 ½ years), *clothed in sackcloth"* (a symbol of humility and repentance). *These are the two olive trees and the two lampstands standing before the God of the earth* (Revelation 11:1-4).

Many people believe these two witnesses will be Moses and Elijah, but this is unlikely because Jesus said Elijah had already come as prophesied (Matthew 17:12-13). Not only that, but if we compare scripture with scripture, we see that the two witnesses (called olive trees and lampstands) are really two *groups* of Christians: Converted Jews and Gentiles (non-Jews).

This is supported by Romans 11:16-18 where we see two groups of people called olive trees: one is good by nature (the Jews), the other tree is wild by nature (the Gentiles). The wild olive branches are grafted into God's good tree, because of their faith in Jesus.

But some of these branches from Abraham's tree— some of the people of Israel—have been broken off (non-believing Jews). *And you Gentiles* (non-Jewish Christians), *who were branches from a wild olive tree, have been grafted in* (Romans 11:17 NLT).

These two groups of believers are *both* part of Abraham's family tree, through his grandson Jacob, who was later renamed Israel (Matthew 1:1-2). Therefore, since Christians have been grafted into Abraham's family tree, all the blessings and warnings given to him apply to the Church too, because they now share the same root system.

Jesus is also from the tribe of Judah (Jacob's son) and also King David, therefore those "in Christ" are also part of His direct lineage, which began with Abraham (Matthew 1:3, 6).

117

Therefore, when converted Gentiles are grafted into God's tree, they are also called the elect.

[Jesus] *united Jews and Gentiles into one people when, in his own body on the cross. He made peace between* **Jews and Gentiles by creating in himself one new people from the two groups** (Ephesians 2:14-15 NLT).

We see this again in other passages. *For you are all children of God through faith in Christ Jesus.* **There is no longer Jew or Gentile,** *slave or free, male and female.* **For you are all one in Christ Jesus. And now that you belong to Christ, you are the true children of Abraham.** *You are his heirs, and God's promise to Abraham belongs to you* (Galatians 3:26, 28-29 NLT).

Young children even sing about this relationship in Sunday School: "Father Abraham had many sons, many sons had Father Abraham. I am one of them, and so are you, so let's just praise the Lord!"

Therefore, the olive tree and the wild branches that were grafted into it are then really two trees joined together as one, because they share the same source, Abraham. Therefore, *If the root is holy, so are the branches* (Romans 11:16).

The apostle Paul made this clear: *Once you were far away from God, but now you have been brought near to him through the blood of Christ. For Christ himself has brought peace to us.* **He united Jews and Gentiles into one people [by]** *his own body on the cross.* **He made peace between Jews and Gentiles by creating in himself one new people from the two groups** (Ephesians 2:13-15 NLT).

We also know that **the two lampstands represent the church**, because Jesus told us so. *The seven stars are the angels of the seven churches, and the seven lampstands are the seven churches* (Revelation 1:20b).

The following scriptures also support the prophecy of the olive trees and lampstands being two *groups* of believers, which are converted Jews and Gentiles (non-Jews).

The prophet Zechariah said, *"I am looking, and there is a **lampstand** of solid gold with a bowl on top of it, and on the stand **seven lamps** with seven pipes to the seven lamps. **Two olive trees** are by it, one at the right of the bowl and the other at its left"* (Zechariah 4:2-3).

The two olive trees (converted Jews and Gentiles) are fueling the lampstands that burn and create the light for the lamps. Jesus also made this clear when speaking to his followers, and said, *"**You are the light** of the world. A city that is set on a hill cannot be hidden. Nor do they light a lamp and put it under a basket, but on a **lampstand"*** (Matthew 5:14-15).

When it becomes obvious that the Great Tribulation is upon us, there will be a worldwide revival and the Word of God will "consume" those who oppose it. *If anyone wants to harm* [these two groups], *fire proceeds from their mouth and devours their enemies* (Revelation 11:5).

This will not be literal fire. It will be the preaching of the gospel where the spoken Word of God is compared to a burning fire. *Therefore, thus says the LORD, the God of hosts, "Because you have spoken this word, Behold, **I am making my words in your mouth fire and this people wood, and it will consume them"*** (Jeremiah 5:14).

119

"Is not my word like a fire?" says the Lord (Jeremiah 23:29).

This bold preaching happens midpoint tribulation. This is when the Antichrist declares that he is God. This is when Satan's full force and fury is unleashed from the bottomless pit and hell literally breaks loose. This is when the mass persecution begins.

This is when everything changes on planet earth.

When [the Christians] *complete their testimony,* **the beast that comes up out of the bottomless pit will declare war against them, and he will conquer them and kill them** (Revelation 11:7).

This is when the global government leader (the Antichrist) and the global religious leader (the false prophet) band together to mandate the Mark of the Beast or be killed for non-compliance (Revelation 13:16-17).

Many who live in free countries today may find it hard to believe that a universal religious leader will someday enforce a global economic order that will exterminate people who don't conform to the rules, but the Bible says that he will (Revelation 13:11-15).

The most powerful religious leader in the world today said, concerning fundamentalists, "Those people are enemies of world peace." This leader was talking about radical religious groups in the Middle East, but many Christians also consider themselves fundamentalist, because they believe in historical Christianity, the inerrancy of the Bible, and the fundamentals of the faith.

Fundamental Christians also believe in the virgin birth and deity of Jesus Christ, His substitutionary death as atonement for sins, His bodily resurrection, and that He will physically return to earth someday. Fundamental Christians believe that Heaven and Hell are both real places, and that angels and demons are both real beings. They believe in moral absolutes, the sanctity of life and that the union between a man and a woman is sacred and instituted by God, and should not be deviated from, no matter what pressure or pleasure comes into one's life.

These beliefs, along with adhering to sound Biblical doctrine, are basic fundamentals of the Christian faith. Will these beliefs someday be grounds for execution?

According to prophecy, the world will think so.

The Great Persecution

The time is coming that whoever kills you will think that he offers God service (John 16:2).

When the two groups of witnesses proclaim the gospel of Jesus Christ, and refuse to submit to the global government and its leader's decrees, the Antichrist and the false prophet will set out to kill them (Revelation 11:7; 13:15-17).

If Christians try to survive under the radar, they may suffer or die from exposure to the elements or lack of basic necessities, since most people are unprepared to live off the grid.

This time of anguish is not only mentioned in Revelation, but also in the book of Daniel. *As I watched, this horn* (leader) *was waging war against God's holy people and was defeating them, until the Ancient One—the Most High— came and judged in favor of his holy people. It will go on for a time, times, and half a time* (3 ½ years). *When the shattering of the holy people has finally come to an end, all these things will have happened* (Daniel 7:21-22; 12:7 NLT).

Horns are symbolic of power and dominance. And just as animals use them for defense and weapons, this leader will wield his power to remove all competition and opposition.

During this time of persecution, seven events then follow:

- *Their dead bodies shall lie in the street of the great city* (Jerusalem), *which spiritually is called Sodom and Egypt, where also our Lord was crucified* (Revelation 11:8).

At the time of John's vision, he never would have compared Jerusalem to Sodom or Egypt, but John was seeing the future and what it looks like today. The Holy city is no longer holy and worldly pleasures abound.

A travel website promoting Jerusalem touts that the city has a thriving and proud LGBT community from all over the world.

Egypt has been considered a hub of worldly pleasures for centuries. Biblical writers have always associated Egypt with the world or worldliness, rather than heaven and holiness.

- *Then those from the peoples, tribes, tongues, and nations will see their dead bodies three-and-a-half days, and not allow their dead bodies to be put into graves* (Revelation 11:9).

This verse is not 3 ½ literal days, but 3 ½ years of persecution, as we read in Daniel's prophecy, and also at the beginning of this chapter where we read that these events will happen for 3 ½ years (Revelation 11:1-4).

This prolonged looking by ALL nations can be done on electronics via satellites, as we gaze at our phones, laptops, and television screens, to view images and videos of past and present events. Never before in history has this phenomenon been possible until these last few decades. Since this massive slaughter will be an ongoing event, it is possible that the news coverage appeared to John as though dead bodies were laying in the streets for a prolonged period of time.

These may also be rerun newscasts like we've seen in historical photos and films such as when Hitler piled bodies in heaps during his evil reign.

- *And those who dwell on the earth will rejoice over them, make merry, and send gifts to one another, because these two prophets tormented those who dwell on the earth* (11:10).

Many people hate Christians and consider them a source of agitation or grief, because of what they believe in and stand for, so when they are killed the world will celebrate their deaths.

- *After 3 ½ days, God breathed life into them, and they stood up! Terror struck all who were staring at them* (11:11).

Again, this is not 3 ½ literal days, but the latter 3 ½ years of Daniel's 70th week, as mentioned earlier. If these witnesses were taken up after 3 ½ literal days, they would not be able to fulfill their 3 ½ year ministry: *I will give power to my two witnesses, and they will prophesy during those 1,260 days* or 3 ½ years (Revelation 11:2-3).

- *Then a loud **voice from heaven called to the two** (martyred) **prophets** (Jews and Gentiles), "Come up here!" And they rose to heaven in a cloud as their enemies watched* (11:12).

A **voice** calls to all the dead in Christ and they are resurrected first. Then, those who are alive and remain meet Jesus in the air. This voice is confirmed in Thessalonians.

*We who are alive and remain until the coming of the Lord **will by no means precede those who are asleep** (dead). For the Lord Himself will descend from heaven with **a shout**, with the **voice** of an archangel, and with the **trumpet** of God. And **the dead in Christ will rise first.** Then we who are alive and remain shall be caught up together with them in the clouds to meet the Lord in the air* (1 Thessalonians 4:15-17).

*In a moment, in the twinkling of an eye, **at the last trumpet.** For the trumpet will sound, and **the dead will be raised incorruptible, and we shall be changed** (1 Corinthians 15:52).*

- *Then the seventh angel blew [**the last**] **trumpet**, and there were loud voices shouting in heaven: "The world has **now** become the Kingdom of our Lord and of his Christ, and he will reign forever and ever." The twenty-four elders sitting on their thrones before God fell with their faces to the ground and worshiped him. And they said, "We give thanks to you, Lord God, the Almighty, the one who is and who always was, for **now you have assumed your great power and have begun to reign*** (Revelation 11:15-17 NLT).

After this it is loudly announced that the kingdoms of the world **now** belong to Christ, since He has returned to rule as King of kings and Lord of lords. Judgment follows, the faithful are rewarded, and the willful are destroyed.

Then Christ's *servants, the prophets and the saints and those who fear* [His] *name, small and great* shall stand in judgment before the Bema Seat of Christ (secure in their salvation) to receive rewards or suffer loss of rewards (1 Corinthians 3:13-15).

- *The nations were angry, and **Your wrath has come,** and the time of the dead, that they should be **judged,** and that You should **reward Your servants** the prophets and the saints, and those who fear Your name, small and great, and should destroy those who destroy the earth* (Revelation 11:18).

We see this time of judgment and reward in other places too, which confirms that this passage is referring to the return of Christ.

The apostle Paul wrote that, **The Lord Jesus Christ will judge the living and the dead at His appearing** *and His kingdom* (2 Timothy 4:1). *And now the prize awaits me—the crown of righteousness, which the Lord, the righteous Judge, will give me **on the day of his return. And the prize is not just for me but for all who eagerly look forward to his appearing*** (2 Timothy 4:8).

In the last chapter of Revelation, Jesus also closes with this promise: *And behold, **I am coming quickly, and My reward is with Me,** to give to every one according to his work* (Revelation 22:12).

Christians may endure a time of hardship and testing, but they will never experience God's wrath, because the wrath takes place after we are raptured (Revelation 11:18).

As mentioned before, confusion arises when Revelation is read in sequential order, when parts of it are actually written as *sidebars or* separate *blocks of time*.

The day of Christ's wrath is the day He returns when the sixth seal is opened (Revelation 6:17). We see this same event described from another angle here in chapter 11. Another description from a different vantage-point is found in Revelation 14:19 and chapter 19. Even though seemingly different, all four views are describing the same event with different details.

Therefore, chapter 11 is an overview of the final 3 ½ years and Christ's return.

Who is the Woman Being Chased by the Dragon?

Revelation chapter twelve contains both history and prophecy, as we see a spiritual panoramic view of the birth of Jesus, His ascension, Satan cast to earth with one-third of his evil angels, and the woman (Israel) fleeing from the dragon who sets out to kill her children (Christians) for 3 ½ years.

Now a great sign appeared in heaven: a woman clothed with the sun, with the moon under her feet, and on her head a garland of twelve stars. Then being with child, she cried out in labor and in pain to give birth (Revelation 12:1-2).

The woman represents Israel. The twelve stars are the children of Israel (Jacob). The child she bears is Jesus. We know this is Israel by comparing scripture with scripture: The sun, moon, and eleven stars are the nation of Israel, because we've already seen this in Joseph's dream when he dreamed of eleven stars (brothers) that bowed to him. Joseph was the twelfth star (Genesis 37:9).

Also, Jesus was not only born in Israel, but he came from the lineage of Abraham, Jacob (Israel), Judah, and David.

And another sign appeared in heaven: behold, a great, fiery red dragon having seven heads and ten horns, and seven diadems on his heads (Revelation 12:3).

The seven-headed red dragon with ten horns is empowered by Satan. The diadems are crowns like those worn by rulers of countries. We also see this same satanic beast in Daniel 7:20-21, and Revelation 13:1; 17:3, 8.

This passage is also mentioned in Isaiah 14 and Ezekiel 28 where both prophets describe Satan's fall from heaven.

His tail drew a third of the stars of heaven and threw them to the earth. And the dragon (Satan) *stood before the woman who was ready to give birth, to devour her Child as soon as it was born* (Revelation 12:4).

Again, the woman symbolizes Israel. Satan tried to kill Jesus after he was born, during the reign of King Herod when he made a decree to kill all the children who were two years old and under (Matthew 2:16).

She bore a male Child who was to rule all nations with a rod of iron (Revelation 12:5). This is referring to the time of Jesus' return and the Millennial reign when Christ rules on earth as King of kings and Lord of lords.

This prophecy is supported by other prophecies that speak of Jesus crushing all rebellion when He returns to rule and reign (Psalm 2:9; Revelation 2:27; Revelation 19:15). The gentle Lamb of God is also the Lion of Judah.

The next verse in chapter 12 is referring to Jesus' ascension (Acts 1:9). *And her Child was caught up to God and His throne* (Revelation 12:5).

Between the time that Jesus ascended to heaven and the coming persecution of Christians, there is approximately a 2,000 year gap in time. (We saw a similar one-verse difference in time with Daniel's seventy weeks prophecy.) Therefore, the remaining verses in chapter 12 refer to future events.

And the woman fled into the wilderness, where God had prepared a place to care for her for 1,260 days (Revelation 12:6). This is another view of the beginning of the 3 ½ year persecution of Christians and Jewish converts.

A spiritual battle in heaven ensues and *the great dragon was cast out, that serpent of old, called the devil and Satan, who deceives the whole world; he was cast to the earth, and his angels were cast out with him. For the accuser* [Satan] *of our brothers and sisters has been thrown down to earth—the one who accuses them before our God day and night* (Revelation 12:9-10).

Prior to this time, spiritual wickedness and evil beings without bodies hovered above the earth in the spiritual realm (Ephesians 2:2; 6:12). But now Satan's boots are on the ground and his evil minions are doing his bidding through the leaders in power.

From this point until the end of chapter 12, events are happening concurrently with chapters 11 and 13. This point in time is the dividing line for everyone in the world, to see who they will follow and who they will obey. For the next 3 ½ years people will be presented with a choice: Submit to Christ or submit to the Antichrist. There will be no other option.

It is imperative that we understand the seriousness of this choice. People must pray and brace themselves for the intense pressure that will take place at that time. This will not only be a life or death situation. It will be an eternal life or death situation, so we must choose wisely, no matter how frightening the thought or how painful the suffering, because this decision will determine the eternal destination of every person on earth.

People must study the Bible *for themselves,* to be nourished in the Word, in order to know the Truth and stand strong at that time (1 Peter 2:2; Hebrews 5:14; John 6:51). This is one of the most important things a person can do to grow their faith, because, *"faith comes by hearing, and hearing by the word of God* (Romans 10:17). We need to build up our courage and fortify our faith and commitment to Christ, because God Himself declared that cowards and unbelievers will not have a part in His heavenly kingdom (Revelation 21:8).

A voice from heaven makes a loud statement, telling Christians how to be spiritually prepared and victorious in the face of persecution: *And they* (Christians) *have defeated him* (Satan) *by the blood of the Lamb and by their testimony. And they did not love their lives so much that they were afraid to die* (Revelation 12:11 NLT).

Believers overcome Satan by claiming the blood of Jesus and by testifying God's Truth. Though these people may physically die, they will live forever in heaven, because they did not deny their faith in Christ, even when faced with death.

When the dragon realized that he had been thrown down to the earth, he pursued the woman who had given birth to the male child (Revelation 12:13). As mentioned earlier, the woman is Israel and the male child is Jesus. Satan then pursues Jewish converts and Christians and tries to kill them. The Dragon (Satan) is the one who empowers the Beast (global government).

*But she was given **two wings like those of a great eagle** so she could fly to the place prepared for her in the wilderness. There she would be cared for and protected from the dragon **for a time, times, and half a time*** (Revelation 12:14).

At one time these eagle wings seemed to have represented the United States, because of her friendship with Israel for years, but this will not happen if America is involved in the global government (the New World Order).

Then the dragon tried to drown the woman with a flood of water that flowed from his mouth (Revelation 12:15). The water here represents people. We know this because in another passage, we are told that the false church sitting upon the water represents people of every language and nation (Revelation 13:1; 17:15). Therefore, it would appear that the water flowing from the dragon's mouth are commands given to his armies to round up the resistors (Christians) and kill them.

But the earth helped her by opening its mouth and swallowing the river that gushed out from the mouth of the dragon (Revelation 12:16).

This may be a counter attack by Israel or an ally who swallows the river (enemy armies) in her defense.

The place prepared for the Jews may also be Petra, which is located in Jordan in Israel. Petra is a fortified ancient city built in the rocks with only one narrow way in and out.

This prophecy was spoken of by Jesus when he warned about the end times. *"When you see the abomination of desolation spoken of by the prophet Daniel, standing in the holy place, then let those who are in Judea flee to the mountains."*

Jesus tells them to run for their lives without stopping to take ANYTHING with them, because the time of persecution will happen quickly and it will be more intense than anything they've ever experienced before (Matthew 24:15-23).

*The dragon was enraged with **the woman, and he went to make war with the rest of her offspring, who keep the commandments of God and have the testimony of Jesus Christ*** (Revelation 12:17).

Satan is only interested in destroying the faithful followers of Jesus Christ. The blasé, half-hearted or self-willed "believers" are not a threat to him, because by their laxity, lukewarmness or rebellion, they are already on his side without even knowing it.

The Lord does not promise His people a life of pleasure, prosperity and ease, but He does promise that they will experience love, joy, and peace from Him, even in difficult times. A life where the end result and destination will be worth every test and trial, because Christ has overcome the world and given us the promise of eternal life in heaven (John 16:33).

The temporary trinkets we cling to here are no comparison to the blessings that await us in heaven.

*Beloved, do not think it strange concerning the fiery trial which is to try you, as though some strange thing happened to you; but rejoice to the extent that you partake of Christ's sufferings, that **when His glory is revealed, you may also be glad with exceeding joy*** (1 Peter 4:12-13).

*For I consider that the sufferings of this present time are not worthy to be compared with the glory which shall be revealed in us (*Romans 8:18).

Eye has not seen, nor ear heard, nor have entered into the heart of man the things which God has prepared for those who love Him (1 Corinthians 2:9).

The Unholy Trinity

Revelation chapter 13 contains some of the most well-known end-time prophecies that people have read and heard. This is where we read about the global government, the Antichrist, the false prophet, the global religious system, the abomination of desolation, the global economy, and the Mark of the Beast (666). Many of these events are also mentioned by prophets in the Old Testament.

The unholy trinity is hell unleashed. It will encompass three great powers that will attempt to unite the world: Satan (in the invisible realm), a global government and its leader, and a global religious system and its leader. These leaders will create an economic network that will monitor and control everyone in the world, simply by tracking their spending.

This is where Satan takes center stage, to counterfeit God the Father, God the Son, and God the Holy Spirit, to deceive the world and set up his own evil empire.

This unholy trinity will be unstoppable until Christ returns.

The Dragon is Satan who empowers the Beast and gives him his authority.

The Beast is the one world government and the Antichrist is its leader. This global system and its leader are often referred to (interchangeably or as a unit) as the Antichrist, but the Last Days *Antichrist will be one specific man* who is in opposition to Jesus Christ (and all that He stands for), because he believes that he is the messiah. He will claim to be the chosen One, the savior and deliverer of humanity, but instead, he will lead many people to their eternal demise, because of his deception.

The False Prophet is the one world religious leader and his organization, who seeks to unite all faiths. But by uniting all faiths, he must omit Christ's death on the cross, as the sacrifice for our sins and His subsequent resurrection. The blood atonement of Jesus Christ and the Truth of His Word will not be in the false prophet's equation, agenda or doctrine. This universal religious leader will also work with the global leader to enforce the Mark of the Beast, because he will be heavily involved in the economy.

The Dragon | Satan Behind the Scenes

The dragon is also called Satan, the devil, and the serpent, and he embodies all that is evil and deceitful. Jesus calls him the father of lies (John 8:44).

One of his methods of deceit is twisting the Word of God, by adding to it or subtracting from it, or by using it out of context, all-of-which create doubt in people's minds concerning the authority of the Scriptures.

We see this subtlety in action when the serpent spoke to Eve and questioned what God had said to Adam. These questions created doubt in Eve's mind, so she countered by adding her own version of what God said. Eve believed the lie and then acted on the faulty information by consuming and then sharing the forbidden fruit with Adam (Genesis 2:17; 3:1, 4).

Casting doubt on the validity of God's Word is how Satan operated in the past. He is using this method in the present, and he will continue to do so in the future. He also has the power to control governments, kingdoms, and empires. We know that he possesses this power, because he tempted Jesus with it in the wilderness.

Then the devil, taking [Jesus] *up on a high mountain, showed Him **all the kingdoms of the world in a moment of time**. And the devil said to Him, "All this authority I will give*

*You, and their glory; **for this has been delivered to me, and I give it to whomever I wish**. Therefore, if You will worship before me, all will be Yours"* (Luke 4:5-7).

Jesus used the Scriptures to overcome Satan when he said, *"Get behind Me, Satan! For it is written, 'You shall worship the Lord your God, and Him only you shall serve"* (v. 8).

Satan wields his power in the spiritual realm, but it also affects the physical world. He is called the spirit prince of Persia and Greece (Daniel 10:20-2), and *the prince of the power of the air* (Ephesians 2:2). He is the ruler of principalities, and powers, and the darkness of this age, and the spiritual hosts of wickedness in the heavenly places (Ephesians 6:12).

Satan will be the power behind the throne during this end time empire. This future human leader wants nothing to do with Jesus Christ, because he wants to rule as savior. He is called the Antichrist, because He is against Christ and wants to take His place. The Antichrist will be the ultimate impostor.

Satan is the temporary ruler of this world, who transforms himself into an angel (or messenger) of light, to deceive people all over the world (John 12:31; 2 Corinthians 11:14-15).

The Beast | The Global Government and its Leader

In Daniel chapter two we read that Nebuchadnezzar had a dream of a huge statue of a man. Daniel interpreted the dream and told the king that it represented five empires. The statue had a golden head, which was symbolic of Nebuchadnezzar and his Babylonian kingdom. The remainder of the body represented future empires: A torso of silver (Persia), a belly and thighs of brass (Greece), and two legs of iron (the Roman Empire). The toes on the feet were made of iron mixed with clay (the end-times empire).

Since the feet and toes are an extension of the legs, many believe that this will be a future revived Roman Empire (iron) that will unite with weaker countries (clay). The ten toes on the feet represent ten kings, or a ten nation federation, which will be the last human-ruled kingdom on earth (Daniel 2:36-43).

These ten toes are also represented as ten horns in Revelation 13:1 and 17:3. Both the toes and the horns represent one-and-the-same group of countries that will unite and rule in the last days' government.

Daniel saw *another* vision of four kingdoms, but this time they are in animal form: **A lion, a bear, a leopard, and a terrifying beast like nothing he'd ever seen before.** They also come out of the sea (Daniel 7:3-8).

Three of these kingdoms have come and gone, but the fourth is yet to arrive. This future beast that Daniel saw was vicious and strong and terrifying. This is the same beast we see in Revelation 13, that will dominate and rule the world for 3 ½ years.

*After this I saw in the night visions, and behold, a fourth beast, dreadful and terrible, exceedingly strong. It had huge iron teeth; it was devouring, breaking in pieces, and trampling the residue with its feet. It was different from all the beasts that were before it, and it had **ten horns.***

*I was considering the horns, and there was another horn, a little one, coming up among them, before whom three of the first horns were plucked out by the roots. And there, in this horn, were **eyes like the eyes of a man, and a mouth speaking pompous words*** (Daniel 7:7-8).

The horns on the beast represent countries or kingdoms with one horn being more prominent and powerful: This notable horn has all seeing eyes and an arrogant mouth. The watchful eyes and boasting mouth represents the Antichrist.

*He **was given a mouth speaking great things and blasphemies**, and he was given authority to continue for forty-two months* or 3 ½ years (Revelation 13:5).

Then I wished to know the truth about the fourth beast, which was different from all the others. I was watching; and the same horn (the Antichrist) *was making war against the saints* (Christians)*, and prevailing against them, until the Ancient of Days came* (the return of Christ)*, and a judgment was made in favor of the saints of the Most High, and the time came for the saints to possess the kingdom* (Daniel 7:19, 21-22).

Daniel saw the end times beast and ruler in his vision. The apostle John saw them too. Both descriptions are one-and-the same government and leader, who will reign during the final 3 ½ years before Christ returns.

The Composite Beast of Revelation 13

The beast (global government) of Revelation 13 also rises out of the water, which represents the sea of humanity (Revelation 17:15). The future beast in the apostle John's vision is a composite of the same three wild animals Daniel saw in his vision. The beast looked like a leopard (known for its speed and ferocious hunting ability) with the feet of a bear (that claw and trample), and the mouth of a lion (that devours).

The character traits of each animal warn us that the global government, while under the Antichrist's rule, will move swiftly, to crush and consume anyone who stands in its way.

*I saw a beast rising up **out of the sea**, having seven heads and **ten horns**, and on his horns ten crowns, and on his heads a blasphemous name. Now the beast which I saw was like a **leopard**, his feet were like the feet of a **bear**, and his mouth like the mouth of a **lion**. The dragon gave him his power, his throne, and great authority. And **I saw one of his heads as if it had been mortally wounded, and his deadly wound was healed. And all the world marveled and followed the beast*** (Revelation 13:1-3).

One of the beast's heads appeared to have died, but the fatal wound was healed. Many people believe this healed head wound represents a partially revived Roman Empire, which today would be the European Union.

The fourth beast shall be a fourth kingdom on earth, which shall be different from all other kingdoms, and shall devour the whole earth, trample it and break it in pieces. The ten horns are ten kings who shall arise from this kingdom. And another shall rise after them; he shall be different from the first ones, and shall subdue three kings. **He shall speak pompous words against the Most High, shall persecute the saints of the Most High,** *and shall intend to change times and law.* **Then the saints shall be given into his hand for a time and times and half a time** (Daniel 7:23-25)

In ancient writings, a time meant one. Times meant two. And a half-time meant half-of-one, which equals 3 ½ years. (This same time-frame is also mentioned in Revelation 11:2-3; 12:6; 13:5).

And all the world marveled and followed the beast. So they worshiped the dragon who gave authority to the beast; and they worshiped the beast, saying, "Who is like the beast? Who is able to make war with him [because it is so powerful]*?"* (Revelation 13:3b-4).

This prophecy tells us that the world will be in awe of the global government and its leader, and they will follow his instructions and obey his mandates.

Yet, Daniel's prophetic overview of the Last Days ends with a message of hope. After this time of intense persecution, Jesus, the King of Kings and Lord of Lords returns to reign forever.

During the reigns of those (last) *kings, the God of heaven will set up a kingdom that will never be destroyed or conquered. It will crush all these kingdoms into nothingness, and it will stand forever. The great God was showing the king* (Nebuchadnezzar) *what will happen in the future. The dream is true, and its meaning is certain* (Daniel 2:44-45b NLT).

The Great Reset

The Last Day's global superpower will rise under the guise of helping humanity, while at the same time imposing limits on what people can own and where they can go. The Great Reset is lining things up for this worldwide utopian society, and their goal is to be fully in place by the year 2030. This New World Order promises benefits that sound helpful at first glance but hidden beneath the surface are ties that bind people to them, which ultimately restricts their freedoms.

Their motto is *Build Back Better*, which in order to do so, something must be dismantled in order to be rebuilt. The World Economic Forum's own website (weforum.org), does not hide this fact. They claim that at this (future) time, "You will own nothing and be happy," because everything will be rented or provided for free.

> "The world must act jointly and swiftly to revamp all aspects of our societies and economies, from education to social contracts and working conditions. Every country, from the United States to China, must participate and every industry, from oil and gas to tech, must be transformed. In short, we need a 'Great Reset' of capitalism" (Klaus Schwab - founder and Executive Chairman of the World Economic Forum).

"The Great Reset will happen with greater speed and with greater intensity than a lot of people might imagine" (John Kerry).

The United Nations is also working toward this unified goal with their 2030 Sustainable Development Agenda. According to the UN website (un.org), we are living in the decade of action, where there is a fervent push to have this agenda in place by the year 2030.

A similar scenario that looks like the Great Reset (the New World Order) is found in Revelation 13, but in this case the government will enforce stricter mandates and will not tolerate anyone who does not conform to their system.

Most of the world will comply with the Beast and the Antichrist. Many will submit to his rules simply because of their desire to survive and keep the status quo. Others will yield due to fear of material loss or fear of death.

The Antichrist will not appear as a red-tailed pitchfork wielding demon. He will be charismatic during the first part of the Tribulation. He will come on the scene by making great promises and boasting great things, but he will turn against Christians when he sets himself up as savior of the world and claims that he is God.

*And he (the Antichrist) was given a mouth speaking great things and blasphemies, and he was given authority to continue for **forty-two months**. Then he opened his mouth in blasphemy against God, to blaspheme His name, His tabernacle, and those who dwell in heaven. It was granted to him **to make war with the saints and to overcome them**. And authority was given him over every tribe, tongue, and nation. All who dwell on the earth will worship him, whose* *names have not been written in the Book of Life of the Lamb slain from the foundation of the world* (Revelation 13:5-8).

This blasphemy against God is the abomination of desolation. This is the starting point of the *Great* Tribulation with three and a half years of turmoil to follow.

This unholy trinity deceives, dominates, and destroys people. Those who submit to the laws of these leaders, may save their lives on earth, but they will lose their souls for eternity.

Below are four distinct points to know about the Beast and the Antichrist.

- This powerful government (the Beast of Revelation) and its leader the Antichrist, are empowered by the dragon, who is Satan (Revelation 13:1-5).

- The ruler of this government, the Antichrist, opposes the one true God (Jesus) and claims that he is God. *He will exalt himself and defy everything that people call god and every object of worship. He will even sit in the temple of God, claiming that he himself is God* (2 Thessalonians 2:4).

- The world "worships" the Beast by bowing to its decrees and receiving its Mark on their hand or forehead in order to buy and sell (Revelation 13:16-17).

- The false prophet works on behalf of the Antichrist, by enforcing the Mark of the government. Those who refuse the Mark will be targeted for destruction, or unable to buy or sell basic necessities to survive (v. 15).

We are seeing previews of this coming purge as Christians are viewed as radicals who need to be "re-educated" (from traditional values). If conservative Christians refuse to get in line with the progressive world agenda, they will suffer the consequences under the mighty hand of the Beast. The global government is already in place and on course to "reset the world" by the year 2030. It is being assembled by the World Economic Forum (WEF), which meets every January in Davos, Switzerland.

The summit's purpose is to connect "key global governmental and business leaders in Davos with a global multistakeholder network in 400 cities around the world for a forward-oriented dialogue driven by the younger generation" (weforum.org).

Professor Klaus Schwab, founder and Executive Chairman of the World Economic Forum said, "The pandemic represents a rare but narrow window of opportunity to reflect, re-imagine, and reset our world."

World leaders are using the global health crisis to move their agenda forward. These changes will not be an overhaul, but a worldwide breakdown of previous norms, in order to *Build Back Better*.

To bring this reset down to a more personal level, *BBB* (the UN agenda) can be compared to how we customize our smartphones, notebooks and laptops when we install our favorite apps, files, and pictures. If something goes wrong with the device, such as a virus (ironic?), or we give it to someone else, we reset it to the factory settings. As soon as we hit the reset button, our identity and preferences are wiped from the device, leaving no trace of who owned the phone or notebook. The phone has no memory of the previous owner's customizations, even if they tried to retrieve it.

In the same way, the Great Reset will not rearrange and save that which we have created to protect our rights and identities. It isn't a fixer-upper of what people have *spiritually* and *morally* believed and lived throughout history. It will be a complete overhaul.

Once these changes are fully in place and aligned with the global economy and the universal ID (Mark), all privacy and rights will be gone.

The Great Reset will change the world as we know it, but it will affect Christians most of all, because of the choice they must ultimately make. The reset will dismantle Biblical principles in order to establish new norms that are in opposition to God's Truth.

Christianity is an exclusive faith because of the atoning death and resurrection of Jesus Christ for sin. The future global government will only allow its all-inclusive religion to thrive, because it aligns with their new liberal system.

The Great Reset promises many social and economic reforms that will benefit humanity, but with these changes, we will lose many of our freedoms as we morph into this one world way of life.

Another group that is working toward this global system is the G20.

The G20 is an international forum that brings together the world's major economies to discuss international economic and financial stability. Its members account for more than 80% of world GDP (gross domestic product), 75% of global trade and 60% of the population of the planet.

The United States may or may not be involved in this end-time global government. It will depend on who is in power at the time. Israel will not be a part of this world system, because the Bible tells us that she will be invaded and half of Jerusalem will be destroyed before Christ returns (Zechariah 14:1-4).

The False Prophet | The Global Religious System and its Leader

Prophets of God are not only those who *see and foretell* the future. They are also the ones who *speak forth* God's Word concerning the future. A *false* prophet, therefore, is one who does not speak with 100% accuracy. Instead, he speaks deceit by adding to or leaving out important truths of the Bible.

The biggest lie the false prophet will promote is not not necessarily something he says, but what he doesn't say. He will omit the crucial message of Jesus' substitutionary death on the cross for our sins. Therefore, we will recognize him not only by his progressive agenda, but also by his silence concerning why Christ came into this world.

Faith in the atoning death of Jesus Christ for sin, and His physical resurrection are the litmus tests of a true prophet, preacher, teacher or believer, because **the salvation of souls was Christ's main purpose in coming to earth**. Verse after verse confirms this:

- *"You shall call His name Jesus, for **He will save His people from their sins**"* (Matthew 1:21).

- *For the Son of Man has come to **save** that which was lost* (Matthew 18:11).

- *For the Son of Man did not come to destroy men's lives but to **save** them* (Luke 9:56).

- *For God did not send His Son into the world to condemn the world, but that the world through Him might be **saved*** (John 3:17).

- *I (Jesus) am the door. If anyone enters by Me, he will be **saved*** (John 10:9).

- *Whoever calls on the name of the Lord Shall be **saved*** (Acts 2:21).

- *Much more then, having now been justified by His blood, we shall be **saved** from wrath through Him* (Romans 5:9).

- *Christ Jesus came into the world to **save** sinners* (1 Timothy 1:15).

Salvation by way of the cross is the invisible hinge on which the door of eternity swings. Repent and receive Christ to be saved. Ignore or refuse His gift and the door swings the other way.

He who believes in Him is not condemned; but he who does not believe is condemned already, because he has not believed in the name of the only begotten Son of God (John 3:18).

It is Jesus' blood atonement, death and subsequent resurrection that proves that He is indeed deity, which makes a way for us to be forgiven and given eternal life. Jesus said, *"I am the way, the truth, and the life. No one comes to the*

Father except through Me. If you had known Me, you would have known My Father also" (John 14:6-7).

The false prophets Jesus refers to are not only those who claim to *be* Christ, but also those who claim to *belong to* Christ, yet preach a false gospel. This is done by leaving the need for Jesus' blood atonement for sin out of the equation. Or, by twisting the Word of God for personal power, gain or glory.

The danger these false preacher's pose is that their message sounds close to the Truth, but it does not align with the scriptures. The Bible calls these people deceivers, false teachers, preachers, or prophets. Jesus calls them wolves in sheep's clothing (Matthew 7:15).

The ultimate impostor will be the universal religious leader during the Great Tribulation who is referred to as *the* false prophet (Revelation 19:20).

A subtle omission or addition to God's Word was how Satan deceived Eve in the Garden of Eden, and tempted Jesus in the wilderness. The serpent created doubt and desire in Eve's mind when he asked, "Did God really say…?"

When seeds of doubt and desire arose in Eve's mind, compromise followed and then the downfall came (Genesis 2:17; 3:1-5). If Satan had blatantly misquoted God, it would have been obvious to Eve. Instead, what he said was *so close to the truth* that she did not spot the difference. She may have also wanted to believe the lie, because there was something in it for her. Her desire to be like God, to decide for herself what was right and wrong was awakened through her senses, while her motivation may have been rooted in pride.

For all that is in the world—the lust of the flesh, the lust of the eyes, and the pride of life—is not of the Father but is of the world. And the world is passing away, and the lust of it; but he who does the will of God abides forever (1 John 2:16-17).

Those who do not believe the Truth are the ones who will swallow the lie. The apostle Paul said, *"I fear, lest somehow, as the serpent deceived Eve by his craftiness, so your minds may be corrupted from the simplicity that is in Christ. For if he who comes **preaches another Jesus** whom we have not preached, or if you receive a different spirit which you have not received, or a different gospel which you have not accepted—you may well put up with it!* (2 Corinthians 11:3-4).

And so it is. The false religious system creates unrepentant, unconverted, unholy "followers" of a different version of Jesus.

The devil challenged Jesus' deity (twice) and quoted scripture to Him: "**If** you are the Son of God" [then prove it by performing a miracle]. The third temptation was to distract Christ from His purpose in coming to earth.

The devil showed Jesus all the kingdoms of the world and their glory, said that he (Satan) would give them all to Jesus, if He would bow down and worship him (Matthew 4:3, 6, 8).

Jesus didn't take Satan's bait. Instead, He quoted Scripture back at the devil, which forced him to retreat.

Knowing the scriptures and using them can also help us resist temptation.

False prophets are notorious for twisting the Scriptures to fit their agenda. This is done through subtle changes to God's Word, which creates doubt or desire, which in turn entices people to believe the lie, and then they are ensnared.

Many people assume that when someone quotes a Bible verse that the person is a Christian with good intentions, but we can see from these examples that this is not always the case. The Bible warns us that *Many corrupt the Word of God* (2 Corinthians 2:17 KJV). This can also be done simply by using the Word out of context, or by selecting key passages to fit their narrative.

The false prophet and his religious system will focus on the temporal and earthly rather than the eternal and heavenly. His ideals will sound wonderful because they benefit humanity, but he will leave out the most important gift of all. Salvation. The Son of God came to earth, to die for our sins, so that we can be forgiven and given eternal life (1 Corinthians 15:3b-4).

Words and phrases such as hell, repentance, redemption through Jesus' blood, salvation by grace through faith in Christ, blood atonement for our sins, and many other fundamentals of historical Christianity, will not be a part of the false prophet's vocabulary or teachings.

The false prophet and others like him will teach humanism and preach that everyone is a child of God, and therefore going to heaven.

The truth is, Jesus Christ *loved us and washed us from our sins in His own blood* (Revelation 1:5). *[And] has delivered us from the power of darkness and conveyed us into the kingdom of the Son of His love, in whom we have redemption through His blood, the forgiveness of sins* (Colossians 1:13-14).

We see more details about this global religious leader in the book of Revelation. *Then I saw another beast coming up out of the earth, and he had two horns like a lamb and spoke like a dragon* (13:11).

The vision of the beast with two horns like a lamb indicates that this is a powerful religious system that speaks deceit like Satan (the dragon), who is the father of lies (John 8:44; Revelation 12:9).

When the false prophet preaches "another gospel," that omits the Truth of Jesus' death and resurrection as atonement for sin, his silence will speak volumes and prove that he is indeed the prophet of deceit (Revelation 16:13; 19:20; 20:10).

When this happens, those who are familiar with the scriptures will know that something is not merely amiss with the false prophet's teachings, but something is very off when he speaks.

*If anyone preaches **any other gospel** to you than what you have received, let him be accursed* (Galatians 1:9).

It is also possible that the two horns like a lamb represent two major religious systems working together, because they both claim the same father (Abraham) as the source of their faith. The idea that these horns may be two religious leaders is supported by other prophetic scriptures

153

that tell us horns represent kings and leaders (Daniel 7:24; Revelation 12:3; 13:1, 17:12).

And [the false prophet] *exercises **all** the authority of the first beast in his presence, and causes the earth and those who dwell in it to worship the first beast, whose deadly wound was healed* (Revelation 13:12).

This powerful religious leader holds the same authority as the first beast (the global government) and he requires everyone to receive the Mark of the Beast in order to take part in the world economic system. The deadly wound that was healed represents the revived Roman Empire, which will come out of the European Union.

He (the false prophet) *performs great signs, so that he even makes fire come down from heaven on the earth in the sight of men* (Revelation 13:13).

This may be actual fire that descends from the sky, since the apostle John knew of at least six other instances in the Old Testament where this occurred, but this could also be a missile or some other type of military fire. Either way, it may be a strong-arm move meant to intimidate people into submission.

False prophets have been around since the time of Moses. Jesus warned his followers about them. The apostles did too, but none of those impostors will compare to the one in power before Christ returns to earth.

It is also possible that the two horns on this beast represent two major sects of Christianity: Progressive Rome and Progressive Protestants. The changes taking place in these two groups may or may not be prophetic in nature, but it does appear that they are laying the groundwork for prophecy to be fulfilled.

What is Progressive Protestantism?

Progressive Protestantism is the compromising church that may be one of the lamb-like horns on this beast. Many in this group that God so loved, deny the crucified Christ of the Bible because the cross speaks of redemption from sin, and sin is not a big deal to them. Although, they do believe in corporate sins, such as neglecting the homeless, or not fighting for women's rights or social equality and justice. But this line of thinking does not bring sin down to a personal level, where one will be individually accountable to God, and thus in need of a savior.

The Bible clearly says, *If we claim we have no sin, we are only fooling ourselves and not living in the truth* (1 John 1:8 NLT).

Progressive Christians believe that Christ is only love and kindness, but if this is true, why did He say that the world hated Him? He gave the answer in the very same sentence: *The world cannot hate you, but it hates Me because I testify of it that its works are evil* (John 7:7).

Therefore, in order to make this sin-loathing version of Jesus more palatable, progressive Christians do not speak of repentance or sin or the need for a savior. They teach and believe that God is not upset with sin, so He is perfectly happy with people just the way they are no matter what they do or how they live.

The Truth is God hates sin, but He loves people so much that he made a way for them to be forgiven and free from its penalty. The Bible says, *For the wages of sin is death, but the gift of God is eternal life in Christ Jesus our Lord* (Romans 6:23).

Many progressive Christians believe in tolerance and support for those who choose to live immoral or sinful lifestyles, even though Jesus never tolerated sin and commanded people to repent. He came to die for sin and spoke out against it, even to the religious leaders: *"You are those who justify yourselves before men, but God knows your hearts. For what is highly esteemed among men is an abomination in the sight of God"* (Luke 16:14-18).

This progressive group ascribes to many beliefs that sound like Jesus' teachings, but they have cherry-picked scriptures and cut away the root of the tree. The foundation of Christianity, which is the cross of Christ and all it represents.

Progressive Christians strive for a sacred unity with all life and believe that Jesus is one of many ways to experience this oneness with life. They also do not believe in absolutes (progressivechristianity.org).

In many ways, Progressive Christianity is similar to the New Age movement. Both groups ascribe to most of the things already mentioned. They also use the name of Jesus, or Christ, or Christ consciousness, to infer that he was a good man, whom we should emulate as a social and moral example like Lincoln, Mandela, or Gandhi.

Both Progressives and those in the New Age movement do not adhere to basic Christian doctrinal beliefs and theology. They do not believe in the authority of the

Bible, the virgin birth, the deity of Jesus or His sacrificial atonement for sin, or that it is necessary to receive Him as Lord and Savior.

Progressive Christians believe they have an evolving faith with a higher and wiser view of God and that Jesus is merely a helpful guide on the path to self-actualization. They "reimagine the scriptures and theology" and they often view the resurrection as a metaphor for personal awakening or enlightenment.

This false religion concept may be difficult for many people to believe, because both groups appear to be genuine with causes that benefit humanity. But if we compare this concept to counterfeit cash, the difference may be obvious to some, but more often than not, the details are small and go unnoticed by the untrained eye.

The only way a person can detect a knockoff is to study the original item. Once they have a thorough knowledge of the genuine, they are better able to spot the forgery. This same idea applies to historical Christianity when compared to progressive Protestantism. If we study God's Word, we will know the Truth and not be deceived by those who twist the scriptures by adding to, or subtracting from them.

False versions of Christianity can be easily found by looking for keywords that are left *out* of their teachings. A few of the words, phrases, or combination of words that you will not see in the progressive vocabulary are sin, destruction, hell, repentance, redemption through the blood of Jesus, substitutionary death as the payment for sin, and justification by faith through the sacrificial death of Jesus Christ on the cross.

Buzzwords in progressive Christianity are phrases such as Jesus awareness, oneness with all life, authentic self, deconstruction of traditional Christianity, and rethinking Christianity. They also believe that we are all children of God by default, therefore they see no need to repent of sin, so it is never mentioned as a step to salvation, since they believe everyone is going to heaven.

Jesus said, *"For God did not send His Son into the world to condemn the world, but that the world **through Him might be saved**. He who believes in Him is not condemned; but he who does not believe is condemned already* (by default)*, because he has not believed in the name of the only begotten Son of God* (John 3:17-18).

The belief mentioned here is not a mere head knowledge of a fact, but a heart belief, receptivity, and dependency on a saving Lord who loved us enough to die in our place.

The flaw of this counterfeit religion and others like it, is that the saving gospel of Jesus Christ has been replaced with the shaky bases of prosperity, humanism, and universalism. These schools of thought are taught worldwide in various churches and they congregate under the umbrella of enlightenment, higher thinking, and hyper-grace.

This new "evolving" interpretation of the scriptures aligns many of its teachings with the New Age and interfaithism. Because of this, the Last Days universal religious system may be a conglomerate of Progressive Christianity and Progressive Rome, to create the interfaith Beast that comes out of the earth with two horns like a lamb, but speaks like a dragon (Revelation 13:11).

158

What is Progressive Rome?

Progressive Rome may also be one of the two lamb-like horns on the Beast in Revelation 13:11. This is because the false prophet's religion will have a universalist doctrine that will leave the gospel of Jesus out of the equation during the process of global unification. This one-size-fits-all religious system will neither recognize Jesus as deity or king, nor will it include His substitutionary death on the cross for sin, so that we can be forgiven and given eternal life.

This is crucial to know, because what Christ did on the cross and His subsequent resurrection are the defining and dividing differences between historical Christianity and all other religions. Therefore, Jesus' atoning death for sin will have no place in this end times unification process.

The church of Rome is not only leaning toward this progressive doctrine, but they are heavily involved in bringing it to pass. An article in the Catholic News Service states that Pope Francis said that *"prayer and crying out to God is the only source of salvation."* He then recommends reading the Psalms for examples of how to pray.

The article does not mention Christ's death on the cross, nor were scriptures such as the following used in the process of explaining salvation through the blood atonement for sin. ***You were not redeemed with corruptible things,*** *like silver or gold, from your aimless conduct received by tradition from your fathers,* ***but with the precious blood of Christ, as of a lamb without blemish and without spot*** (1 Peter 1:18-19).

The pope does not mention the name of Jesus, or sin, or salvation by grace through faith in Christ at all in this article. The pope's lack of inclusion is silently denying the reason Jesus came to earth, which is to *save His people from their sins* (Matthew 1:21). *Christ* [did this when He] *suffered once for sins, the just for the unjust, that He might bring us to God* (1 Peter 3:18).

Mohammad, Buddha, the pope, nor any other person can make this claim. Jesus is the One and only Messiah, who forgives sin and gives us eternal life in the presence of God the Father (John 14:6).

In the push for global unity, religious leaders are using Abraham as their common source of faith, to create peace in the Middle East, and to unify religions all over the world.

> The United Arab Emirates unveiled plans this weekend for an interfaith complex in Abu Dhabi that will **unite a church, a synagogue and a mosque**. The announcement of the three houses of worship, collectively known as the "Abrahamic Family House," follows Pope Francis' February visit to the UAE, the first papal visit to the Arabian Peninsula. During the visit, Pope Francis and the grand imam of al-Azhar, Dr. Ahmed el-Tayeb, **signed a declaration to form an interfaith council called The Higher Committee of Human Fraternity** (Fox News, September 24, 2019).

In the "Document on Human Fraternity for World Peace and Living Together," signed by Pope Francis and the Grand Imam, we can see (by doing a word search) that the name

Jesus is not mentioned once, nor are the words sin, repent, atonement, cross, resurrection, heaven, hell, surrender, obedience, sanctification, nor any other words that are relevant to salvation, or the result of salvation through Christ. The Document also states:

> We, who believe in God and in the final meeting with Him and His judgment, on the basis of our religious and moral responsibility, and through this Document, **call upon ourselves, upon the leaders of the world as well as the architects of international policy and world economy,** to work strenuously to spread the culture of tolerance and of living together in peace.

Pope Francis does not spread the gospel of Christianity and repentance, but rather a gospel of unity, humanity and tolerance. On the contrary, Jesus said His message would divide people, even those in their own home. *"Do not think that I came to bring peace on earth. I did not come to bring peace but a sword. and a man's enemies will be those of his own household"* (Matthew 10:34, 36).

The Pope's *Document on Human Fraternity and Peace* appears to be the new foundation of faith. It contains lists of ideas and values that will supposedly bring souls to salvation.

> We call upon intellectuals, philosophers, religious figures, artists, media professionals and men and women of culture in every part of the world, to rediscover the values of peace, justice, goodness, beauty, human fraternity and coexistence in order to

confirm the importance of **these values as anchors of salvation for all,** and to promote them everywhere.

No Jesus. No acknowledgement of sin or repentance. No mention of eternal life by grace through faith in Christ, but the Pope does call upon various people of all walks of life, to rediscover the values listed above **as anchors of their salvation**.

Jesus' blood atonement on the cross is our anchor of salvation, not a list of values. God's infallible purpose in Christ is the *hope we have as an anchor of the soul.* It is *Jesus,* [who is our] *High Priest forever* (Hebrews 6:19-20).

The *Last Days* religion will be a false Christianity, an unfaithful bride, because it leaves Jesus and his purpose for coming out of the equation. If everyone is going to heaven by default then why did Jesus have to die?

He died because we are all sinners and the eternal destination of our souls was at stake. Without the blood atonement for sin and the resurrection of Christ, there is no hope of heaven and eternal life.

We are all sinners. Therefore, we cannot enter heaven on our own merit, nor stand in the presence of a holy God based on our own goodness, because all *our righteousnesses are like filthy rags* in comparison (Isaiah 64:6). We are hopeless without Christ, and therefore we need Him as Savior (Ephesians 2:12). *For there is one God and one Mediator between God and men, the Man Christ Jesus* (1 Timothy 1:5).

Without Christ, *No one is righteous.* We have *all sinned and fall short of the glory of God* (Romans 3:10, 23). But in His love, God provided a perfect sacrifice in His Son, as payment for our sins. The Bible says, *This is real love—not that we loved God, but that he loved us and sent his Son as a sacrifice to take away our sins* (1 John 4:10 NLT).

There is a wide chasm between what the Bible says about Christianity and what the pope says about humanity. He is very involved in social, political, economic, and ecological matters, and believes that all people are children of God, no matter who they are or how they live.

Pope Francis believes that the way to promote the economy and education is "finding the courage to place the human person at the centre" (Vatican News).

Jesus Christ is the central focus and foundation of the Christian life, not people.

The pope is using every means possible to advance his ideology except the most important tool one would assume a religious leader would use, which is seeking spiritual guidance and wisdom from the Bible, to advance God's kingdom.

Progressive Rome is also "Re-educating" young people. The pope wants to empower them through education, because they are the future. This education is more of a re-education to the ways of the new global order. This "opportunity" opens the door to promote progressive Christianity, which states that Jesus is a good moral example, whom we emulate in our lives.

There is no mention of sin or God's judgment against sin, because progressive Christianity believes that there is no judgment. This belief teaches that everyone is basically good at their core, whereas the Bible states the opposite. *The heart is deceitful above all things, and desperately wicked* (Jeremiah 17:9).

Progressive Rome is also very involved in the economy. During the pandemic, the pope held a virtual event for people aged 35 and under from around the world, to share ideas on how to make the present and future economy balanced and sustainable for everyone on the globe.

At the event, time was allotted for meditation and reflection from texts of literature and poetry, along with art, music and talks from various speakers from all over the world.

The itinerary made no mention of prayer or Scripture reading as a guide to implement his plan. Instead, Pope Francis is looking to Saint Francis of Assisi as an example to guide them.

The Pope also has his own website called, the *Economy of Francesco* (EoF), where he states that *Young economists, entrepreneurs, and changemakers,* [are] ***giving a new soul** to the economy.*

This all sounds very pious and nice, but the pope has taken the focus off Christ and the cross at Calvary, and put the focus on Saint Francis, the unity of all religions, and feeding the poor by redistributing wealth.

What good does it do to feed a body, to extend a life on earth, but then starve a soul for eternity, by not telling them the Truth about Jesus as Savior? Rome has taken a soft stance on the ultimate purpose of Christ coming to earth, which was not to advocate for economic and environmental reforms, but to die for the sins of the world.

The meetings of Pope Francis are noble causes indeed, but Jesus and His purpose for coming to earth as Savior are not mentioned once in the itinerary. Again, this is because the pope believes and teaches that everyone is a child of God, no matter what they believe or how they behave.

The Vatican website quotes him as saying, "The *status quo* should be replaced by giving education 'a long-term vision,' to create a new humanism," as he promotes a "new universal solidarity" (Vatican News). Humanism is defined as an outlook or system of thought attaching prime importance to **human rather than divine matters**.

The pope is also promoting the idea that the "stewardship of common goods (freedom from possessions) should be placed at the center of teaching in schools, university and business schools."

> We feel the need for young people who, through study and practice, know how to demonstrate that a different economy exists. "What if the economy of *sine proprio* **(without possessing or without property) was that of the era of common goods? Will it be the *oikonomia* (economy) of Francis that will save both us and the earth in the end?"**

We don't know who the false prophet will be until the time arrives, but these statements are something to think about, since the false prophet will be the one who endorses the Antichrist and enforces the Mark of the Beast (Revelation 13:16-17).

Ultimately, the end time global religion will focus on promoting life on earth, rather than a focus on promoting souls to heaven by pointing them to the historical version of Jesus Christ.

Past and Future Persecution

Whoever the false prophet may be, he will not only be instrumental in uniting all religions, but he will also be deeply involved in political and social issues and the world economic situation. He is also the one who enforces the Mark of the Beast. He places all focus and dependency on the one world leader and his global economic system, along with his own politically based church, rather than Jesus Christ and His kingdom.

These two systems work together to sift out those who resist their authority and refuse to receive the Mark. God will also use these leaders and their decrees to sift the true believers from the indecisive or half-hearted believers. This new economic system will shake those sitting on the fence, so they will land on one side or the other, depending on their own choosing (Hebrews 12:27; Revelation 3:10b).

It may be hard to believe that a religious leader would turn against Christians and have them killed, but it has happened in the past, and the Bible says that it will happen again in the future.

Many of the chief priests and the Pharisees hated Jesus and wanted to have him killed. After Jesus raised Lazarus from the dead, they pushed even more for His demise and eventually they succeeded (John 11:47, 53; 18:3).

History also tells us that during the Inquisition, the Catholic church tortured, maimed, and killed (often by burning at the stake or hanging), up to 300,000 "heretics," over the course of four hundred years, all in the name of eliminating what they considered heresy. Some of their victims were the Knights Templar, Joan of Arc, Protestants, Jews, Muslims and more.

The Inquisition was a powerful office set up within the Catholic Church to root out and punish heresy throughout Europe and the Americas. Beginning in the 12th century and continuing for hundreds of years, the Inquisition is infamous for the severity of its tortures and its persecution of Jews and Muslims. Its worst manifestation was in Spain, where the Spanish Inquisition was a dominant force for more than 200 years, resulting in some 32,000 executions [of Spanish Protestants] (History.com).

These people were not killed for refusing to conform to the *Bible,* but for refusing to conform to the *man-made teachings* of the Roman church. We can easily see that at various times throughout history, leaders have implemented religious uniformity by force. Those who didn't conform were considered heathens and then persecuted, tortured, or martyred.

We are seeing precursors of this today with the Ecumenical Movement pushing for multi-faith unity all over the world. This unification process teaches and preaches universalism, which means everyone is going to heaven, no matter what they believe or how they behave.

In the Last Days, all faiths will be tolerated by the Antichrist, *except historical Christianity.* The political and religious leaders will leave Christ's death on the cross for sin, and His physical resurrection out of his global church, to promote the new "Messiah" (the Antichrist) and his interfaith movement.

Even today, people label those who don't waver in their faith, misled, intolerant or a threat to society, because they don't yield to pressure and conform to their progressive thinking and ways.

Beware lest anyone cheat you through philosophy and empty deceit, according to the tradition of men, according to the basic principles of the world, and not according to Christ (Colossians 2:8).

The wisdom of this world is foolishness with God (1 Corinthians 3:19).

We are on the throes of a world that will soon be shaken, as we move at a rapid pace toward the time of testing. Those who refuse the mark will be unable to buy or sell anything, because money will be worthless. These non-conforming Christians will be forced to live off the grid, or they will be killed or die a natural death, because they will not be able to obtain things they need to survive.

This deprivation and persecution will be so intense that people will betray one another to save their own lives. They will also betray one another due to unbelief, sin-hardened hearts, or fear of material loss or social standing.

Jesus said this would happen: *You will be betrayed even by parents and brothers, relatives and friends; and they will put some of you to death. And you will be hated by all for My name's sake. But not a hair of your head shall be lost. By your patience possess your souls* (Luke 21:16-19).

Jesus also said, *The time is coming that **whoever kills you will think that he offers God service**. And these things* *they will do to you because **they have not known the Father nor Me*** (John 16:2-3).

We don't know for sure who the false prophet will be, but the stage is being set for the universal religious system and its leaders to take center stage.

For such are false apostles, deceitful workers, transforming themselves into the apostles of Christ. And don't marvel for Satan himself is transformed into an angel of light. Therefore it is no great thing if his ministers also be transformed as ministers of righteousness (2 Corinthians 11:13-15).

What is the Mark of the Beast

This may be the first chapter you turned to if you scanned the table of contents. If so, it may be because the Mark of the Beast is one of the most well-known prophecies in Revelation, even among non-Christians. There seems to be a curiosity and fascination concerning this subject, because books and movies have even been made about this topic.

The problem is there is not a lot of information or clarity about it out there. Therefore, if you turn to no other section in this book except this chapter, I urge you to keep reading so you will know exactly what the Bible says about this matter. The primary scriptures concerning the Mark of the Beast are found in Revelation 13:1-18.

In a nutshell, the "Mark" of the "Beast" will be some type of personal identification embedded in a person's hand or forehead that will also be tied to his or her bank account, which will then be monitored by the World (Central) Bank. The Mark will be mandated by the global government and the global religious system (the two Beasts) in order for people to function in society.

The soon-to-be universal ID will be used like debit cards are today. The difference is the future chip will be *in* the person instead, so it will be with them at all times. It will also contain personal information and a tracking device just like we have in our smartphones.

The technology is already in place to form a cashless society. This alone is powerful proof that Bible prophecies are true. There is no way the apostle John could have imagined a worldwide economic system with such accuracy back in 95 A.D., except that God gave him the vision to warn us today.

Yet here it is, lining up before our eyes and in our foreseeable future.

For simplicity sake, I will often refer to the Mark of the Beast as the MOB or the chip. The future Mark will be a computer chip, or Real ID, or RFID (Radio Frequency ID) implant, or some other form of microchip embedded under the skin.

It may be introduced into society for the purpose of vaccination status or something similar, in order to create trust and familiarity, so the masses will become desensitized to it.

Today when we make purchases with debit or credit cards or QR codes, they are forms of e-currency or digital currency, but they are obviously not the MOB. **The Mark of the Beast will be recognized by three very distinct things. Anything other than these three things are NOT the Mark of the Beast of the Bible.**

- The Mark of the Beast will not be in place until **3 ½ years after** the peace treaty with Israel is signed.

- The Mark of the Beast will be the ONLY way that a person will be able to buy or sell, because cash will be completely eliminated.

He causes all, both small and great, rich and poor, free and slave, to receive a mark on their right hand or on their foreheads, and that no one may buy or sell except one who has the mark or the name of the beast, or the number of his name (Revelation 13:16-17).

- The Mark of the Beast will require every person to acknowledge the Antichrist as God, Savior, or the Messiah (which means that in doing so, they must deny the One true Savior, Jesus Christ, in the process), and submit to this leader's global mandates.

[When] *the man of lawlessness is revealed, the son of destruction, [he] opposes and exalts himself against every so-called god or object of worship, so that he takes his seat in the temple of God,* **proclaiming himself to be God** (2 Thessalonians 2:3-4).

Another part of this mandate may be that people will be required to accept the new norms and morality that are contrary to God's Truths and absolutes. But those who deny Christ's teachings will also be denying Christ.

*For whoever is ashamed of **Me and My words**, of him the Son of Man will be ashamed when He comes in His own glory, and in His Father's, and of the holy angels* (Luke 9:26).

They worshiped the beast, saying, "Who is like the beast? Who is able to make war with him?" (Revelation 13:4).

Worship does not necessarily mean *in awe* of someone or something. It also means loyalty, devotion, or yielding one's will to another's authority, such as in the case of this leader and his government.

The Mark of the Beast will therefore be the mark of the government, which will be tied to the central banking system. Its precursor is scheduled to launch in the near future. When the Central Bank Digital Currency (CBDC) is fully in place, we will become a cashless society.

This will not be the Mark of the Beast, yet. The three things that were previously mentioned must first take place: Peace in the Middle East for 3 ½ years. The world leader must take center stage proclaiming he is god. Currency must be eliminated in all countries affiliated with the global government, and the new means of buying and selling with the Mark (electronic device) will take its place.

The future MOB will be tied to the World Bank and it will be promoted as a good thing. It will not only be a convenient way to make purchases, but a cashless society will also eliminate a lot of crime. Tax evasion, bank robberies, drug deals, human trafficking, working off the books, counterfeiting cash, and other illegal money related activities will be nearly impossible to carry out without getting caught, because the chip will monitor all transactions through a central banking and tracking system.

Of course, some of these crimes will still take place under the guise of fake business transactions, or through bartering systems where precious metals, gems, and other merchandise and services are traded. But overall, the extent of illegal activity will be minimal in comparison with what it is today. This digital system will also expose hidden stashes of cash, since money will need to be put in the bank and converted to electronic currency, or lost forever.

The Central Bank Digital Currency is a mass government monetary and surveillance system that is being tested in major countries around the world. When this system is available everywhere, it will end all financial (and thus lifestyle) privacy, because all purchasing information will be in real-time for their all-seeing eyes to monitor.

This means that other forms of privacy will also be impossible, because the (eventual) microchip will pinpoint a person's exact location whenever and wherever they make a transaction. It will also record everything they have purchased (thanks to 5G tech).

This invasion of privacy will be promoted as a way to help humanity by making life easier and eliminating crime, when in reality it is a form of control because the government will know our every move.

*And **he causes all**, both small and great, rich and poor, free and slave, **to receive a mark on their right hand, or on their foreheads, and that no one may buy or sell, except one who has the mark** or the name of the beast, or the number of his name* (Revelation 13:16-17).

The Apostle John saw the hand and forehead as the location of the mark. He knew nothing about computer chips, fingerprints, eye scans, or facial recognition. He had no clue of technology, so he wrote what he saw: the hand, the forehead and the eye area, as a means the Mark uses to make transactions.

Here is wisdom. Let him who has understanding calculate the number of the beast, for it is the number of a man: His number is 666 (Rev 13:18).

Scholars have discovered that the word *Beast* and the name *Nero Caesar* both calculate to the number 666 when using Hebrew numerology (gematria). Nero blamed Christians for setting Rome on fire, so he crucified them and then used them as human torches to light his garden parties. He also threw Christians to wild animals or made torturous sport of them in the arenas, as a way to have them killed.

During intermittent times of the Roman Empire some emperors allowed Christians to live as long as they acknowledged that he was God. Citizens were required to bow to the emperor's image, toss a pinch of incense into a fire and then proclaim, "Caesar is Lord!" Many who refused lost their ability to buy and sell in the marketplace, but most were tortured and killed.

In his vision, the apostle John compared the Last Days government in Revelation to how life was during Nero's brutal rule. The 666 that John mentioned was his way of writing in code, to warn us that a future ruler like Nero will be in power during the last 3 ½ years of the Great Tribulation.

The Verichip or "Real ID" came on the scene in the late 1980s. It began as an identification device that was inserted under the skin of a person's pet. This marker could then be scanned to extract the chip ID and medical information, if the animal was ever lost, stolen, or injured.

A few years ago, people began being chipped too, but this is *not* the Mark of the Beast. The future Mark will be extremely different. It will require a person to make a clear definitive choice to either bow to the government, or to stand for Christ (Revelation 13:7-8). There will be no middle ground.

This decision will not only determine what happens here on earth, but also what happens later in heaven. The choice made here at that time will determine a person's eternal destination.

Those who choose the Mark of the Beast will literally be selling their souls to Satan and sealing their eternal fate (Revelation 14:9-11).

Who Wants the MOB in Place?

Political and religious leaders, among many other influential people, are pushing for a universal e-currency and a universal basic income (UBI). The false prophet will hold a tremendous amount of power in this upcoming political co-reign, since he is the one who will enforce the Mark of the Beast.

Shortly after the Antichrist declares that he is God (the abomination of desolation), he and the false prophet will impose the cashless society. Prototypes of this system are already in place as we move toward this end with the use of digital currency. This money may also be called cybercash, digital dollars, or some other name associated with *electronic* transference of funds.

The religious leader's goals will be more focused on "global" issues than heavenly matters. The props are in place and Pope Francis is paving the way for this end-time leader to take center stage. He is a globalist who is against global-warming. He promotes global citizenship, a global education alliance, a global compact on education, and a global change of mentality through education. He has also created his own global economic plan called *The Economy of Francesco* (francescoeconomy.org) where he chooses only young people (under 35), to be a part of his program and covenant, to build a new normal on "sister earth."

Revelation 13:12-15 explains what the false prophet will do while working with the political ruler.

He (the religious leader) *exercises all the authority of the first beast* (the world government and its leader) *in his presence, and causes the earth and those who dwell in it to worship* (obey) *the first beast, whose deadly wound was healed* (the revived Roman Empire / European Union).

He performs great signs, so that he even makes fire come down from heaven on the earth in the sight of men (possibly fireworks as a celebration, or missile fire as a warning).

He deceives those who dwell on the earth by those signs which he was granted to do in the sight of the beast, telling those who dwell on the earth to make an image to the beast who was wounded by the sword and lived. (The false prophet tells people to create the image that will be tied to the beast / government economic system).

He was granted power to give breath to the image of the beast, that the image of the beast should both speak and cause as many as would not worship the image of the beast to be killed. (Modern technology will make this possible, while the progressive mindset will enforce the decree.)

What are Precursors to the MOB?

Precursors of the Mark of the Beast are already in place and are being used today under various names. The verichip, RFID (Radio Frequency ID), RAIN RFID (RAIN also stands for RAdio frequency IdentificatioN). The latter microchip is much smaller and faster than the verichip (which is the size of a grain of rice). These trial runs are conditioning people to accept the future Mark.

The electronic world is charging full speed ahead to make this new way of living possible. We see an example of how the electronic currency will be used if we look at Sweden (a country with 10 million people). Sweden is a 99% cashless society with 6,000 of those people being chipped for buying and selling purposes. More recently, Sweden has added a Covid vaccine passport to their implant for easy verification.

Another place that has experimented with hand scans is River Falls, Wisconsin where they have used chips to bypass electronic logins and traditional keys. Select businesses in the United States are also using the chip to track employee productivity. The US, Sweden and Wisconsin experiments are not the Mark of the Beast, but they (and other test runs) are precursors of the one to come.

The Verichip (or something similar) is a possible precursor of the Mark. The ultimate purpose of the MOB will be tracking and control with the added benefit of eliminating fraud, flight, and crime.

Countries currently moving toward a cashless society are Finland, China, South Korea, the UK, Australia, the Netherlands, and Canada. Moscow released their new facial recognition system, "Face Pay," that allows people to pay for rides on the metro, simply by looking at the camera as they pass through the turnstiles.

Amazon One recently rolled out a "Pay-by-Palm" plan that allows shoppers in physical stores to pay for items by placing their palm over a scanning device. This is done after the initial linking of a credit card to a person's palm print.

This whole idea of a chip implant containing purchasing info is not so far-fetched when you consider that we are already using debit card chips, barcodes and QR (Quick Response) codes with ATMs, scanner wands and cell phone cameras.

A currency change being implemented by the Federal Reserve will be called FedNow accounts. This new banking system will allow all purchases, payments, deposits and withdrawals to be done in real time from business to business, person to business, and person to person (24/7/365 uninterrupted processing) with the same immediacy as cash.

These real-time transactions will then leave an immediate electronic footprint that can be monitored and tracked anywhere, anytime. The first phase of FedNow is expected to be up and running by 2023.

Another step toward the MOB is tracking and surveillance technology, which is readily available and easily obtained by the average citizen. Many people have CCTV (closed circuit television) security and surveillance cameras and monitors at their homes and businesses to view events live and then archive footage for later retrieval and reference.

According to IHS Markit (a data provider in London), over 1 billion surveillance cameras have been installed globally as of 2021. These CCTVs are everywhere: Schools, stores, gas stations, restaurants, parking lots, streetlights, and various other places. Many are disguised so they are not detected by the average passerby. Paradise Valley, Arizona, has installed license-plate readers in fake cactuses to check plates against a national database of stolen vehicles.

A precursor to the Mark may be used for verifying vaccinations, or for finding a lost child, or a wayward Alzheimer's family member, or for capturing an elusive criminal. It may eventually contain personal information, such as a birth certificate, driver's license, passport information, work or criminal history, credit report, or medical records.

Whatever the future Mark of the Beast is, it will be so shocking to Christians that *there will be no mistaking it.*

How Will the Mark be Implemented?

All the world marveled and followed the beast (Revelation 13:3).

The Mark of the Beast will come on the scene as a solution to many of the world's problems. Everything from medical contact tracing, to controlling crime, to buying and selling, to the government handing out funds, will all be handled electronically through the chip.

This all sounds like a good thing, but a trade must be made to receive these benefits. The exchange will be that one must forfeit many long-held freedoms and beliefs and then be accountable to the world government for everything.

The Mark of the Beast will be a way to keep people in line with government regulations and rules. The United Nations Development Program website states that they have set the date for the agenda 2030 (undp.org) to meet their Sustainable Development Goals (SDG).

The Pope is also pushing for a universal basic income wage. Both groups share the common goal of ending poverty by siphoning revenue from the wealthy and sharing it with the poor. This Universal Basic Income may be one of the benefits the Antichrist dangles for those hesitant to receive the Mark.

Another way to recruit people may be fear. Under normal circumstances many people would not voluntarily receive the MOB, but broadcast daily pandemic or war statistics and one raises the fear factor ante, while promises of contact tracing to keep one safe may be a motivation.

Aside from the fear of dying from the virus, people were afraid of starving to death or running out of paper products during the pandemic. We saw this fear play out when shelves were emptied due to panic buying. The Mark could be a way to control rations which would prevent excessive buying and hoarding. Many people in a panic will submit to just about anything to be safe or to get their fair share.

The powers behind the Great Reset are gauging public response for future reference, by studying their reaction during the ebb and flow of the pandemic. When the panic and pressure lessens, and people let down their guards, society *will not* return to its previous state of normalcy, because the "new normal" has already been established.

Then, when another disaster comes along, the world's agenda will pick up where it left off and move forward again until we become accustomed to the latest version of the new normal.

This lack of reaction and retraction is similar to a frog in warm water that acclimates to its surroundings. If you put a frog in hot water, it will immediately leap out. But if you put that same frog in lukewarm water and then gradually turn up the heat, it will stay in the water until it boils to death.

In this same line of progressive movement, currency will gradually be phased out as we transition solely to debit cards, then QR codes to scan on phones, and then to body-chips as people come under the watchful eyes of the globalist monitoring system.

This is not so far in our distant future. China is quickly moving ahead to becoming a cashless society. This means that the United States and other countries will be forced to use digital currency if they want to do business with them. Or they may jump on board simply to compete or to keep up with the times.

The Federal Reserve is already looking at digital currency for the United States. Analysts believe that America will have a digital currency issued by the Federal reserve within the next few years. *"About 90 countries are exploring or launching their own* (Central Bank Digital Currencies) *CBDCs"* (Bloomberg.com).

When digital dollars are in place via the chip, currency as we know it will be as worthless as Confederate money after the Civil War. Paper and coin currency will be a thing of the past.

What is the Image of the Beast?

This image will not be a golden calf or a Nebuchadnezzar style statue that people will bow to on bended knees. That would be too obvious and therefore rejected by many people. It would also be unrealistic to think this leader would build a giant talking statue and place it in the middle of a major city for all the world to see and to worship. This would not be logical either, because many people around the world would not be able to travel to that particular location, to personally give allegiance to the image.

The image of the beast could be something conjured up in the Metaverse Virtual World or in a 3D hologram with speech cloning capabilities that appears and speaks in various places. This type of deception may play a part in the Antichrist role, but VR or a 3D hologram would not be an effective way to enforce the Mark.

The "image" will most likely be something we are already familiar with and using every day such as a media screen, because that is the only way *everyone, everywhere* would be able to see the image, hear it speak, and "worship" it. Whereas if the image was a huge statue, it would have to remain parked in one place, and most people who live in various locations of the world would not be able to travel to see, hear, and worship the image.

A screen or monitor would allow billions of people to see the political and religious leaders speaking to the masses and telling them what to do, but there is a problem with this concept too. People may see the image and hear it speak on a screen, but those in charge behind the scenes would not know if a person was actually "worshiping" the image of the beast (government) or not complying, so **there must be some other connection**.

The way to keep track of those who have received or refused the Mark of the government is through the electronic use of buying and selling, as mentioned in Revelation. All purchases, no matter how big or small, will be tracked electronically through the use of the Mark (chip implant) and then transmitted to a universal database, such as the World Bank. This buying and selling will then be monitored by the Beast (the government, Central Banks, or the World Bank) and the Antichrist's all seeing eyes (Daniel 7:8).

The image is what is *on the screen itself*, along with its audio capability which allows it to speak before or after scanning a purchase or making an online transaction. This is how the beast will enforce the ability to buy or sell, or allow the demise of those who don't comply. Those who refuse the Mark will simply not be able to use the economic system.

The apostle John saw in his vision that [The false prophet] *was granted power to give **breath** (life) **to the image of the beast, that the image of the beast should both speak** and cause **as many as would not worship the image of the beast to be killed.** He causes **all, both small and great, rich and poor, free and slave**, to receive a mark on their right hand or on their foreheads, and that no one may buy or sell except one who has the mark or the name of the beast, or the number of his name* (Revelation 13:15-17).

Since John had never seen a media screen, it may have appeared to him that the image was alive, because it could speak and appeared to move. He did not understand what he was seeing in his vision because he had nothing to compare it to, so it's possible that the closest thing he could relate to was seeing someone worshiping an idol.

When a person worships an idol they **face the image, bow their head** in reverence, and then **stretch out their hand(s)** in prayer, or to offer a sacrifice to the false god.

This is similar to *what it appears* people are doing at self check-outs in stores, or while shopping online even now. When a person makes a purchase, they lower (bow) their head to **look at the product image** and the cost of the item on the media screen. They may hear the audio component give instructions (automated or a facetime-type interaction) to complete their transaction, and then scan their **outstretched hand** (with the implanted chip) to pay for their items.

These actions would all appear to John as a form of worship or bowing to an image, since he had no idea what screens, monitors, or scanners were during the first century.

All these things will not happen in some distant future. Precursors are being tested now and will be refined in time, because those involved in the Great Reset are arranging the stage and the technology is already in place.

5G High Speed Internet

*This little horn had **eyes like human eyes** and a mouth that was **boasting arrogantly*** (Daniel 7:8).

The little horn mentioned in the book of Daniel is the last day's leader and his system that will monitor people on a global scale. The amazing thing about the Mark of the Beast prophecy is that it could not have been implemented even a few decades ago, but it is now possible to "see" and collect data on everything and everyone through 5G technology and satellite tracking.

The difference between 4G and 5G tech is speed and accuracy. This immediacy of tracking must be available when the MOB is in place.

> 5G is expected to offer network speeds that are up to 100 times faster than 4G LTE and reduce latency to nearly zero, it will allow networks to handle 100 times the number of connected devices, revolutionizing business and consumer connectivity and enabling the "Internet of Things" (The National Law Review).

4G technology can locate a person within a one mile radius, but 5G can pinpoint a person's exact location. An article appeared in *Fast Company* (March 2019) explaining how 5G will not be like the "Eiffel Towers" of the past, but small antennas that will be "dotted around on rooftops and street lights and inside shopping malls and other buildings."

> "Anyone with access to your ISP's cell tower data will be able to hone in on **your exact location** far more precisely than they can today under our 4G networks... As you move through a city, **your mobile network provider will be able to chart the path you take with a high degree of accuracy** since your device will keep jumping from connecting to one nearest 5G tower to the next...You're going to see a lot more indoor towers–in shopping malls, big office buildings, hotels and so on" (FastCompany).

When people receive the MOB during this end-time empire, it won't be a phone signal big tech is tracking, it will be the chip in a person's hand. Phones can be lost or left behind. A chip implant cannot be separated from its owner, because once embedded, it becomes a permanent part of the person who receives it.

The horn of Daniel and Revelation, with its all-seeing eyes, will know every move a person makes, as every transaction is viewed, tracked, monitored, and regulated by a centralized security system such as the CBDC (Central Bank Digital Currency) and / or the World Bank.

Everyone who has the Mark will leave an electronic footprint or a paperless paper trail. The global government will know what everyone is doing, where they are located, what they are buying, and what they are selling. And if the government does not like any of these things, they can shut down a person's chip as a form of control or punishment. This will be done with "programmable" digital currency that is designed with built in controls that can specify what a person can or cannot buy or where they can or cannot go.

These ID chips will not only give authorities information, but social media platforms have already gathered huge amounts of data from us. Facebook has our photos for facial recognition. Apple phones have our fingerprints. Ancestry has our DNA. And we have made known our likes, dislikes, interests, political views and religious beliefs on most social platforms and search engines such as Google. It would be difficult for many of us to get lost in the crowd when we have voluntarily given up so much personal information.

This invasion of privacy and personal tracking is possible today more than ever before in history. Cameras and microphones with face, voice, and gait recognition (through Artificial Intelligence) will be connected to these high speed towers to keep everyone under their watchful gaze.

The Beastly government of Revelation will know everyone's business and location. That is unless you're one of the few who live off the grid, but even that will be difficult to do, because of the *Internet of Things*.

The Internet of Things

When all 5G towers are in place, their signals will pick up every "thing," because everything will have its own ID tracking number and it will be traceable everywhere at all times.

The Internet of Things (IoT) will not only connect people (who have the chip) to the Central Banking system's database, but it will also connect people to *objects in* their possession, because the two devices will always be in communication with one another.

At this very moment, over 20 billion connected "things" are gathering information, relaying messages to each other and performing tasks all over the world. "Things" such as heart monitors, smart watches, appliances, drones, and robots, among other items.

As more satellites go up, there will be no connection dead zones. The 5G plan is to eventually launch 30,000 to 42,000 satellites to orbit the earth within the next few years (Forbes 2020/01/30). This will make it possible for IoT surveillance devices to be placed in remote locations without wired connections.

When this happens, the whole world (minus the Arctic regions) will have access to technology and the Internet, which also means that **technology will have access to everyone and everything** in the world. When these tracking devices are in place, they will always be on and the government will know everyone's habits, preferences, desires, strengths, and weaknesses, simply by monitoring the places they go and the things that they buy.

Should a person decide to bug out and live off the grid and have someone smuggle food or supplies to them from the store, the food or item will have its own unique ID and therefore, your friend and also the location of where he took the food may be traced. The only way to possibly prevent food or merchandise tracking may be to remove all labels and packaging, that is unless there is an embedded chip in the product.

If these methods don't succeed in flushing out those who don't comply, drone flybys with heat sensors may spot people in remote areas, or Starlink's constellation of satellites will find a person's location if they have any type of electronic device in their possession. Because of this, it will be very difficult for the average person to suddenly become invisible and self-sustaining in the wilderness.

Though this food traceability seems far-fetched, it's already made its way into the grocery and retail businesses. Walmart, Nestle and Tyson are just a few of the companies already on board with the IoT to ensure food safety and transparency for the consumer by tracking the product's journey from farm, to store, to checkout lanes.

When the world gets to the point where the chip is the only way to buy and sell, people will betray one another out of fear of loss. When there is a threat to their own lives and survival, desperate people do desperate things to keep themselves alive.

Jesus predicted this would happen. Family members will even betray one another to the death. The Bible says, *Now brother will deliver up brother to death, and a father his child; and children will rise up against parents and cause them to be put to death* (Matthew 10:21).

All globalist countries involved with the revived Roman Empire (EU) will be affected by the Mark of the Beast. Israel will not be a part of this network and economic system. We know this because Israel will be persecuted by the Beast.

Prophecy states that the Jewish people who don't conform will be killed for non-compliance. Jerusalem will also be invaded at the end of the Tribulation period by surrounding countries (most likely Russia, China, Turkey, and /or Iran) before the Second Coming of Christ (Ezekiel 38-39; Daniel 11:40-41; Zechariah 14).

The Mark of the Beast will be the ultimate means of control. Everything necessary to make this possible is already in place. The coming global government and its economic and social system will control people by "helping" them through the redistribution of wealth, but there will be a fallout with this free-for-all. The receivers will then be monitored by the givers, who control the economic valve through which the income flows.

This global government is also called the New World Order, the Great Reset, or the Beast of Revelation.

What Happens if You Take the MOB?

Those who don't get the Mark, don't get to use the system. Therefore, fear of loss and the threat of death will motivate people to comply. The desire for immediate peace and safety will override many people's thoughts of eternal security, and therefore, motivate them to receive the Mark.

As frightening as this time will be, it is crucial to remember that the eternal consequences are not worth the exchange and temporary time of well-being. The Bible says, *What we suffer now is nothing compared to the glory he will reveal to us later* (Romans 8:18 NLT).

For those who receive the MOB, life will continue in the new normal for a very short time (3 ½ years). Those who submit to the global government will be able to buy, sell, travel and receive medical help with greater ease than ever before, because with a swipe of the hand, or a scan of the forehead, everything is done.

Those who receive the MOB, but don't comply with the global government's rules and regulations, may be controlled by the electronic device in his or her hand. Basic needs may be rationed out, suspended, or terminated if a person does not follow their mandates.

Not long after receiving the MOB, something else will happen to these people. Those with the Mark will experience so great a pain that they will wish that they were dead.

The Bible states that the locusts [which may be helicopters or military drones], *Were commanded* [to harm] *only **those men** [and women] **who do not have the seal of God** on their foreheads. And they were not given authority to kill them, but to torment them for five months. **Their torment was like the torment of a scorpion when it strikes a man.** In those days **men will seek death and will not find it; they will desire to die, and death will flee** from them* (Revelation 9:4b-6).

The word "strike" in this verse is translated, "to sting (to strike or wound with a sting)" such as one would experience from an injection or an insect sting (Strong's G3817).

A similar or ongoing issue occurs later in Revelation. Those who received the Mark will experience some type of painful infection. The Bible says, *A foul and loathsome sore came upon **the men** [and women] **who had the mark of the beast and those who worshiped his image.** They gnawed their tongues because of the **pain.** They blasphemed the God of heaven because of **their pains and their sores,** and **did not repent of their deeds*** (Revelation 16:2, 10-11).

We see that those who experience this pain don't turn to God, but curse Him instead. As bad as these descriptions are, they are all temporary consequences compared to the eternal result of receiving the Mark. In the end, those who choose to yield to the Antichrist's authority and receive the Mark will suffer for eternity.

*If anyone worships the beast and his image, and receives his mark on his forehead or on his hand, he himself shall also drink of the wine of the wrath of God, which is poured out full strength into the cup of His indignation. **He shall be tormented with fire and brimstone in the presence of the holy angels and in the presence of*** *the Lamb. And the smoke of their torment ascends forever and ever; and they have no rest day or night, who worship the beast and his image, and whoever receives the mark of his name* (Revelation 14:9-11).

This is such a serious matter that God would not allow a person to flippantly or unwittingly receive the Mark. Something significant will take place at this time that will cause people to sit up and take notice. This decisive event will be so glaring and obvious that people will recognize that something dramatic is happening.

And in the end at the final judgment, the fate of the corrupt leaders is clear. *The beast was taken, and with him the false prophet that wrought miracles before him, with which he deceived them that had received the Mark of the Beast, and them that worshiped his image. These both were cast alive into a **lake of fire** burning with brimstone* (Revelation 19:20).

Those who have no faith or deny their faith in Christ and submit to the MOB will lose their souls in the end. Receiving the Mark is the point of no return. Eternal damnation is their destination. Therefore, it is crucial to know the Truth (Revelation 14:9-11).

Therefore, no matter what happens, *DO NOT UNDER ANY CIRCUMSTANCES RECEIVE THE MARK OF THE BEAST, EVEN IF IT MEANS DEATH.*

A person may think, "I'll secretly believe in Jesus Christ AND take the Mark to survive," but that will not be possible.

[Jesus said], *For whoever desires to save his life will lose it, but whoever loses his life for My sake and the gospel's will save it. For what will it profit a man if he gains* the whole world, and loses his own soul? Or what will a man give in exchange for his soul? For **whoever is ashamed of Me and My words** (my teachings) in this adulterous and sinful generation, **of him the Son of Man also will be ashamed when He comes in the glory of His Father with the holy angels** (Mark 8:35-38).

Jesus also said, This is *the hour of trial which shall come upon the whole world, **to test those who dwell on the earth*** (Revelation 3:10b).

This time of testing will sift the grain from the chaff. The choice regarding the Mark of the Beast will reveal what is in a person's heart: What they believe, who they love, and who they truly follow. As difficult a time this will be, the purpose of these trials is to bring people to repentance and faith in Christ.

*Many will be **purified, cleansed, and refined by these trials.** But the wicked will continue in their wickedness, and none of them will understand* (Daniel 12:10 NLT).

When confronted with this time to choose, there will be no more half-hearted people who casually say they are Christians. No sorta, kinda, maybe, sometimes believers, or "I think Jesus was a good teacher or role model" type answers. No, a person either believes that Jesus Christ is the Son of God, who died for their sins and then physically rose from the dead...or they do not. The Antichrist will only offer two choices: His way or death. There will be no in-between.

We do not know when the Mark will be mandated or how it will unfold, but it would be wise to repent and receive Christ as Savior now, to be prepared for this future time. Salvation begins with a humble and contrite heart, as we believe in Jesus and then ask Him to save us.

Jesus said, *"Assuredly, I say to you, unless you are converted and become as little children, you will by no means enter the kingdom of heaven. Therefore whoever* **humbles himself** *as this little child is the greatest in the kingdom of heaven"* (Matthew 18:3).

We cannot let ego, intellect, or willfulness stand in the way of His gift of forgiveness and eternal life. For there awaits a never-ending life of love, joy, peace, beauty and bliss for those who humbly receive Him as Lord.

If you confess with your mouth the Lord Jesus and believe in your heart that God has raised Him from the dead, you will be saved. For with the heart one believes unto righteousness, and with the mouth confession is made unto salvation. For **"whoever calls on the name of the Lord shall be saved"** (Romans 10:9-10, 13).

If you are a Christian, but have become lukewarm, the same message of repentance applies. Jesus said, *"I know your works, that you are neither cold nor hot. I could wish you were cold or hot. So then, because you are lukewarm, and neither cold nor hot, I will vomit you out of My mouth* (Revelation 3:15-16).

The startling part about this text is that these Christians were IN the body of Christ. A person cannot vomit something out that was not there in the first place.

But Jesus is not done with these people. He tells them to turn around, open the door and let Him inside, so that they too, will know love and joy in His heavenly kingdom.

As many as I love, I rebuke and chasten. Therefore **be zealous and repent**. *Behold, I stand at the door and knock. If*

195

anyone hears My voice and opens the door, I will come in to him (Revelation 3:19-20).

What Happens if You Don't Take the MOB?

A person will never accidentally or unknowingly receive the Mark of the Beast, nor will they be fooled or forced to receive it, nor will it be hidden in a medical injection. When the actual Mark of the Beast comes on the scene, a defined line will be drawn in the sand by the global leader and the false prophet concerning historical Christianity. When the MOB becomes mandatory, a person must either believe that the Antichrist is God and receive the Mark, which will allow them to buy and sell, or believe that Jesus Christ is God, and not take the Mark.

This decision will have eternal consequences: Take the Mark and live for a while, but suffer for eternity. Or refuse the Mark and physically die, but live forever in heaven. Those who choose to lose their lives on earth will retain their souls for eternity. And like Job, they will be able to say, [God] *knows the way that I take; When He has tested me, I shall come forth as gold* (Job 23:10).

Christ clarifies what following Him truly means during this time of tribulation. *Then Jesus said to His disciples, "If anyone desires to come after Me, let him deny himself, and take up his cross, and follow Me. **For whoever desires to save his life will lose it, but whoever loses his life for My sake will find it**"* (Matthew 16: 24-25).

A person carrying a cross has no goals and they're not going back to the life they once lived, because they are walking to their death. Therefore, we carry our cross and die to ourselves by doing His will, not ours.

Jesus continues by telling us that this life or death decision will be presented to believers before He returns.

*"For what **profit is it to a man if he gains the whole world, and loses his own soul?** Or what will a man give in exchange for his soul? For the Son of Man will come in the glory of His Father with His angels, and then He will reward each according to his works"* (Matthew 16:26-27).

When confronted with the choice of whether to take the MOB or die, this passage becomes more clear that it is referring to the Tribulation period, since Jesus immediately speaks of His return and reward. The choice given is to gain the world (its necessities and comforts), but lose our souls in exchange. Or, lose what the world has to offer and gain eternal life instead.

Those on the fence must settle this decision and make up their mind whose side they are on. The Holy Spirit will provide courage and strength during these difficult times.

*Blessed are those who are persecuted for righteousness' sake, for theirs is the kingdom of heaven. Blessed are you when they revile and persecute you, and say all kinds of evil against you **falsely** for My sake. Rejoice and be exceedingly glad, for great is your reward in heaven, for so they persecuted the prophets who were before you* (Matthew 5:10-12).

The Bible makes it clear that this will be a time of testing. And just as a refiner uses fire to extract the genuine from the dross, these trials will serve the same purpose.

*You have been grieved by various trials, that the **genuineness of your faith**, being much more precious than* *gold that perishes, though it is **tested by fire**, may be found to praise, honor, and glory **at the revelation of Jesus Christ*** (1 Peter 1:6b-7).

*Beloved, do not think it strange concerning **the fiery trial which is to try you**, as though some strange thing happened to you; but rejoice to the extent that you partake of Christ's sufferings, that **when His glory is revealed, you may also be glad with exceeding joy*** (1 Peter 4:12-13).

Those Who Stood in the Face of Death

Those who confess that Jesus is Lord must prepare themselves to take a stand without wavering, because believing that Christ is Lord will be a threat to the Antichrist, who believes that *he* is God. And he will not compete with Jesus for anyone's devotion.

Many Christians will be persecuted and killed for non-compliance to the Beast, yet there will be survivors during this time until Christ returns (Revelation 11:9-10; 13:15; 18:4, 23).

We know this because the Bible tells us that, *We who are alive and remain until the coming of the Lord will by no means precede those who are asleep. Then we who are alive and remain shall be caught up together with them in the clouds to meet the Lord in the air. And thus we shall always be with the Lord* (1 Thessalonians 4:15-17).

The word *"remain"* in these two verses is translated from the word *perileipomai*, which means "survive" (Strong's G4035). This word is only found twice (in this unique form) in the entire Bible. Therefore, if we read these two verses again with the original text, they say, *"We who are alive and* [survive] *until the coming of the Lord ... We who are alive and* [survive] *shall be caught up together with* [the dead in Christ] *in the clouds to meet the Lord in the air.*

This is why it is important to become as self-sufficient as possible. It would be wise to stock up on non-perishable food, plant a vegetable garden, invest in solar panels, a generator, and possibly a water filtration system. It would also be wise to purchase things that can be used to barter with others. Offering one's skills may be another way of exchanging goods and services.

Yet the Bible is still clear that those who refuse the Mark may be martyred for their faith or die of starvation, dehydration, illness, or exposure, because they will not be able to buy or sell as they had previously done.

[This persecution] *shall be for a time, times, and half a time; and when the power of* **the holy people has been completely shattered,** *all these things* **shall be finished.** (Daniel 12:7).

This time-frame in Daniel coincides with Revelation 16:17 when the angel pours out the last judgment just before Christ returns.

*Then the seventh angel poured out his bowl into the air, and a loud voice came out of the temple of heaven, from the throne, saying, "**It is done!**"*

Christians may experience suffering for a while, but they are assured of eternal life no matter what physically happens to them. This is because when Christ returns, they will be resurrected with new and perfect bodies that will never perish.

So what are we to do? It is crucial that we settle this in our hearts and minds before we are faced with the decision concerning the Mark. We must choose Christ and keep living for Him through the power of the Holy Spirit, *no matter what happens to us on earth.*

This seemingly impossible task of standing for our faith has been carried out with courage in the past. Three captive men in Babylon were once confronted with a mandate to worship an image of gold or die, but they courageously stood for their faith instead. In this case God miraculously delivered them.

Shadrach, Meshach, and Abedgego answered and said to the king, "O Nebuchadnezzar, we have no need to answer you in this matter. If that is the case, our God whom we serve is able to deliver us from the burning fiery furnace, and He will deliver us from your hand, O king. **But if not, let it be known to you, O king, that we do not serve your gods, nor will we worship the gold image** *which you have set up"*
(Daniel 3:16-18).

Daniel refused to give up his daily time of prayer when the king signed a degree that it was illegal to do so. Daniel not only prayed his usual three times a day on bended knees, he also did it by his window where they could clearly see. Because of this, Daniel was thrown into a den of lions but miraculously emerged unhurt. The king was so impressed with Daniel's deliverance that he became a believer and prophesied about God's kingdom.

I [King Darius] *make a decree that in every dominion of my kingdom men must tremble and fear before the God of Daniel. For He is the living God, and steadfast forever; His kingdom is the one which shall not be destroyed, and His dominion shall endure to the end* (Daniel 6:26).

An eternal perspective and an eye on the prize is what motivated Moses to leave a life of power and prestige.

By faith Moses, when he became of age, refused to be called the son of Pharaoh's daughter, **choosing rather to suffer affliction with the people of God** *than to enjoy the passing pleasures of sin, esteeming the reproach of Christ greater riches than the treasures in Egypt;* **for he looked to the [future]** **reward** (Hebrews 11:24-26).

During the 3rd century in the Roman province of Carthage, Perpetua and Felicity were two young Christian women who had both recently given birth when they (and three men) refused to renounce their faith, or toss a pinch of incense to the false god and proclaim, "Caesar is Lord."

Perpetua was born into a wealthy family, and because of this, her father had arranged for her release if she would simply offer a pinch of incense or recant, but she refused.

Instead, she boldly proclaimed, "Above all else, I am a Christian!" She made it known to all that she served a living God and His name was Jesus Christ.

Once inside the area, Perpetua raised her hands in a song of joy, as though claiming her victory over Satan. And the men boldly preached to the spectators, "Flee from the wrath to come! Today you are condemning us, but one day God will condemn you!"

When it came time for them to dress in robes in honor of the pagan gods before they were martyred, Perpetua said, "We do this of our own free will and come to die for Christ, not for your gods." And they were not made to change their garments.

The five who died that day, displayed great faith and peace before they were slain by wild animals and the sword. The keeper of the prison, who had watched over Perpetua and her friends, was so impressed with their faith that rather than becoming fearful after witnessing their suffering and death, he became a Christian instead.

At Perpetua's request, the jailor completed what she had begun writing in her diary. He wrote that on the day she and her friends walked to the arena, *They went forth from the prison into the amphitheater as it were into heaven, cheerful and bright of countenance; if they trembled at all, it was for joy, not for fear. And then they began to sing.*

In some cases, Christians were divinely protected, but in most cases they were killed. Many other men and women throughout history have stood for their faith, even though it cost them their lives. The twelve apostles were all persecuted and eleven of them died as martyrs. John, the writer of Revelation, was tortured before being exiled to the Isle of Patmos, but he was the only one who later died a natural death. In the book of Acts we read about Steven who was stoned to death. The apostle Paul was beaten many times and even left for dead before he was eventually beheaded in Rome.

Christians were periodically persecuted by the Roman government. They were made sport and spectacles in the arenas when they were thrown to lions or ripped apart by similar vicious animals. Others were dragged, beaten, burned, beheaded or crucified without wavering, because they knew a more glorious reward awaited them in heaven.

Throughout the centuries men and women have also suffered similar fates.

Those who are spiritually born-again have the assurance of eternal life, and that everlasting life began the moment they believed and received Christ as Savior. A Christian's body may be killed, but their soul will never die. And whether living or dead, all believers will someday meet Jesus in the air to receive resurrected, glorified bodies that will never perish (John 3:16; 1 Corinthians 15:51-52).

Here is the patience of the saints; here are those who keep the commandments of God and the faith of Jesus. Then I heard a voice from heaven saying to me, "Write: 'Blessed are the dead who die in the Lord from now on'" (Revelation 14:12-13).

These Tribulation martyrs will be given a full reward in the kingdom of God (2 John 8), along with the assurance that they will never hunger, thirst, or feel the heat of the sun again (like they did while suffering during the Tribulation), because Jesus will feed them and lead them to living waters, and God Himself will wipe the tears from their eyes (Revelation 7:16-17; 21:4).

When Hell Literally Breaks Loose

The Abomination of Desolation ushers in the *Great Tribulation* with 3 ½ years of turmoil to follow. This is the beginning of the second half of the seven year tribulation, also known as the time of Jacob's (Israel's) trouble.

Revelation chapter 13 is the third concurrent view of the 3 ½ years of persecution of those who refuse the Mark of the Beast. The other two chapters that warn of this time are Revelation 11 and 12, along with the fourth and fifth seals (Revelation 6:7-11).

The abomination of desolation that Daniel was referring to was when Antiochus Epiphanes IV, who ruled Palestine from 175-64 B.C. set up an altar for Zeus in the temple and offered a pig as a sacrifice. Daniel also saw another abomination that would take place in the future. This future desecration will take place when the world leader (the Antichrist) enters the temple, halts the daily sacrifice, and declares to the Jews that he is their long-awaited Messiah (God).

The king will do as he pleases, exalting himself and **claiming to be greater than every god**, *even blaspheming the God of gods* (Daniel 11:36 NLT).

This is the event that Jesus refers to in Matthew 24:15-21. This is the event the apostle Paul also refers to in 2

Thessalonians: *He* (the Antichrist) *will exalt himself and defy everything that people call god and every object of worship.* **He will even sit in the temple of God, claiming that he himself is God** (2:4 NLT).

The Antichrist will be one of the many signers or designers of the peace treaty with Israel. He is the man of peace mentioned when the first seal is opened. He is the rider on the white horse who will (figuratively) gallop out of the European Union or another neighboring country (Revelation 6:2).

In the middle of the seven years (after the agreement is signed), he will change course, break the peace agreement with Israel, and then stand in the holy place and declare that he is God, and therefore should be worshiped.

He was given a mouth speaking great things and blasphemies, and he was given authority to continue for forty-two months (3 ½ years). Then he opened his mouth in blasphemy against God, to blaspheme His name, His tabernacle, and those who dwell in heaven.

It was granted to him to make war with the saints and to overcome them. And authority was given him over every tribe, tongue, and nation. **All who dwell on the earth will worship him, whose names have not been written in the Book of Life of the Lamb** *slain from the foundation of the world* (Revelation 13:4-8).

This is when the Mark of the Beast will be introduced and enforced. This will be a time of great suffering for those who refuse to submit to his world government and global economic system, as confirmed in the book of Daniel.

It shall be for a time, times, and half a time (3 ½ years); and when the power of the holy people has been completely shattered, all these things shall be finished... from the time that the daily sacrifice is taken away, and the **abomination of desolation** *is set up, there shall be one thousand two hundred and ninety days,* which is 3 ½ years (Daniel 12:7, 11).

Peace with Palestine may be the key treaty that unlocks this prophecy, because the Bible tells us that the Jews and Palestinians will be sharing land in Judea (the West Bank) during this time.

Jesus also described how the prophecy will unfold when the treaty is broken.

"Therefore when you see the **'abomination of desolation,'** *spoken of by Daniel the prophet, standing in the holy place, then* **let those who are in Judea flee to the mountains.** *Let him who is on the housetop not go down to take anything out of his house. And let him who is in the field not go back to get his clothes"* (Matthew 24:15-18; Mark 13:14, 19).

Once the Antichrist breaks the peace agreement and declares that he is God, chaos soon follows. Those in Judea must immediately flee, because the invasion and devastation will be swift. Those outside their homes are warned not to go back inside to even get a coat. Instead, Jesus said they must run for their lives, because the persecution will be so great (Matthew 24:16-25).

His (the Antichrist) *power shall be mighty, but not by his own power* (Satanic influence)*; He shall destroy fearfully, and shall prosper and thrive; He shall destroy the mighty, and also the holy people* (Daniel 8:24).

The Antichrist will pursue Christians and conquer them (Daniel 7:21). This is an ongoing persecution that begins 3

½ years into the Tribulation and ends when Jesus returns to conquer evil and set up his kingdom on earth (Revelation 11:7; 13:7). Details concerning this mass persecution and devastation were mentioned earlier in the chapters, "The Two Witnesses," "The Woman and the Dragon," and "What Happens if You Don't Take the MOB?"

Daniel gives more details concerning what the Antichrist and his government will be like. *This horn had seemed greater than the others, and it had human eyes and a mouth that was boasting arrogantly. As I watched, this horn was waging war against God's holy people and was defeating them, until the Ancient One-the Most High-came and judged in favor of his holy people. Then the time arrived for the holy people to take over the kingdom* (Daniel 7:20-22).

The eyes on the horn may represent surveillance cameras and tracking devices that will be everywhere during the Antichrist's reign of terror. The arrogant, boasting mouth will be this leader's blasphemies against God when he proclaims that he is the savior (Rev 13:5-6; 2 Thessalonians 2:3-4). This is until the Almighty One returns and intervenes with His saints to claim His kingdom.

Christians may not know the day or hour of Christ's return, but once these events take place, they can estimate the time-frame of the Second Coming. This is because we are told that when the Abomination of Desolation and other key events take place, Christ will return 3½ years later (Revelation chapters 11, 12, 13; Daniel 12:11).

Watch therefore, for you do not know when the master of the house (Jesus) *is coming—in the evening, at midnight, at the crowing of the rooster, or in the morning—*

lest, coming suddenly, he find you sleeping. And what I say to you, I say to all: Watch!" (Mark 13:35-37).

Now learn this parable from the fig tree: When its branch has already become tender and puts forth leaves, you know that summer is near. So you also, when you see all these things, know that it is near—at the doors! (Matthew 24:32-33).

The Six Events Before Christ Returns

Revelation chapter 14 is an *overview* of six events that will happen shortly before and when Christ returns. The 144,000 with Jesus, the three angels who each give a message, and then the harvest of the righteous and the harvest of the unrighteous.

First, we see the 144,000 sealed Jewish converts standing with Jesus on Mount Zion. *They are virgins. These are the ones who follow the Lamb wherever He goes. These were redeemed from among men, being firstfruits to God and to the Lamb* (Revelation 14:1, 4).

Zion always refers to Jerusalem, the City of David, or the Temple Mount. *Blow the trumpet in Zion, and sound an alarm in My holy mountain! Let all the inhabitants of the land tremble;* **For the day of the Lord is coming, For it is at hand** (Joel 2:2).

These converted Jews are called virgins, which means they are faithful followers of Christ (Revelation 14:4). It may be possible that these men represent both the Christians and converted Jews who were martyred and then resurrected. Again, this is possible because Jesus referred to His followers as virgins in the parable of the wise and foolish virgins (Matthew 25:1-13). It is also possible that these men represent both groups, because Christians and Jews share the same ancestral root system in Abraham's family tree, as mentioned earlier.

We also see that these 144,000 are called the firstfruits of the Lamb, which mean they are Tribulation martyrs who have been resurrected by Christ (1 Thessalonians 4:14-15). We know these ones have been resurrected, because they are not referred to as souls. They are physically *standing* with Jesus in Jerusalem (Revelation 14:1-5).

We also know there will be Christians who are alive at this time, because the earth has not yet been reaped. The great harvest happens a few verses later in Revelation chapter 14:14-20.

This scenario is entirely possible because the dead in Christ are resurrected first, *before* those who are alive in Christ. The Bible says, *We who are alive and remain until the coming of the Lord will by no means precede those who* [have died] (1 Thessalonians 4:15).

After this, we see three angels appear on the scene who relay three different messages.

The first angel gives a final altar call to the world before the hour of judgment falls. The angel proclaims the *everlasting gospel to those who dwell on earth-to every nation, tribe, tongue, and people-saying fear* (reverence) *God and give glory to Him, for **the hour of His judgment has come.** Worship Him who made heaven and earth, the sea and springs of water* (Revelation 14:6-7).

This passage shows us that there will be people who survived the Tribulation period. Those who have made it to this point and desire the gift of eternal life, must turn to Jesus

Christ and ask Him to save them. The Bible promises that *whoever calls on the name of the Lord shall be saved* (Romans 10:13).

The second angel proclaims that Babylon the great city (the location of the political and / or false religious system that rules over the world) has fallen and is destroyed. *Another angel followed, saying, "**Babylon is fallen, is fallen,** that great city* (Revelation 14:8).

The details of this city and its destruction are also described in the chapter, "The Wealthy City Burns" (Revelation 18). Since the wording in chapters 14 and 18 are identical, we can surmise that these two descriptions are the same event.

In Revelation chapter 18, the angel says, *"**Babylon the great is fallen, is fallen,** and has become a dwelling place of demons, a prison for every foul spirit, and a cage for every unclean and hated bird!* (v. 2).

The third angel gives a powerful warning about submitting to the beast (global government) and receiving his Mark: *"**If anyone worships the beast and his image, and receives his mark on his forehead or on his hand, he himself shall also drink of the wine of the wrath of God,** which is poured out full strength into the cup of His indignation.*

He shall be tormented with fire and brimstone in the presence of the holy angels and in the presence of the Lamb. And the smoke of their torment ascends forever and ever; and they have no rest day or night, who worship the beast and his image, and whoever receives the mark of his name" (Revelation 14:9-11).

Jesus drank the cup of God's wrath when he died on the cross, so that we would not have to drink it (Matthew 26:39, 42, 44: John 18:11). Those who reject His gift of grace will one day drink this cup themselves.

The third angel then addresses Christians and explains what will happen to them and how to stand firm in their faith when facing persecution. *This means that God's holy people must endure persecution patiently, obeying his commands and maintaining their faith in Jesus* (Revelation 14:12).

This command is similar to the one that was mentioned in Revelation 13. *Anyone who is destined for prison will be taken to prison. Anyone destined to die by the sword will die by the sword. This means that God's holy people must endure persecution patiently and remain faithful* (v. 10).

This aligns with Jesus' command for us to be wise as serpents and harmless as doves (Matthew 10:16). The writer of Hebrews made a similar statement when he said, ***Patient endurance*** *is what you need now, so that you will continue to do God's will. Then you will receive all that he has promised. "For in just a little while, the Coming One will come and not delay. And my righteous ones will live by faith. But I will take no pleasure in anyone who turns away"* (Hebrews 10:36-38 NLT).

Those who are alive during this time are told they must patiently maintain their faith in Him (Revelation 14:12). This can be done by speaking the name of Jesus Christ and proclaiming His blood over evil beings we cannot see. The disciples discovered this truth when they said, *"Lord, even the demons are subject to us in Your name"* (Luke 10:17).

Using Christ's name or claiming His blood over a situation forces evil to flee. [The Christians] *defeated* [Satan] *by the blood of the Lamb and by their testimony. And they did not love their lives so much that they were afraid to die* (Revelation 12:11 NLT).

We are also told to stand firm in our faith and refuse to submit to things contrary to God's Word. The Bible says, *Blessed is the man who remains steadfast under trial, for when he has stood the test he will receive the crown of life, which God has promised to those who love him* (James 1:12).

Christians must refuse to become bitter in the face of persecution or death. When we get to the point where we can say, "Not my will, but thine be done," we receive a peace that passes understanding, even in the midst of hostility.

This is the ultimate test of faith. One that will be difficult to carry through unless a person is fully yielded to the Holy Spirit. This total abandonment to God allows His Spirit to empower us during the time of testing. And as strange as this may sound, the inner-peace that Christians exude may motivate unbelievers to receive Christ when they see our courage and faith.

This happened in the early church when Christians were sporadically persecuted and martyred over the course of two centuries. Many of them entered the arenas with dignity, courage and strength. Some walked out with lifted hands while singing and praising God. They did these things as they were whipped, imprisoned, crucified, burned alive, torn apart by wild animals, fed to lions as sport, and tortured to death in other horrific ways.

Yet, their great faith, courage and conviction was so evident that it aroused admiration of many unbelieving spectators. As a result, some of those who watched the Christians suffer or die for their faith, became believers in Christ themselves.

The very movement the government tried to crush began to grow instead: *"There were pagans present at these martyrdoms who were so impressed by the courage of the Christians that they came to see the truth of the Christian religion themselves and immediately converted to Christianity"* (PBS.org).

This historical fact is also confirmed by the Christian theologian Tertullian, when he said, "The blood of the martyrs is the seed of the church."

These Christians were able to respond in this way because they were spiritually prepared. They did not cower or fight, because they were so sure of their eternal destination that they were willing to give up their temporary residence on earth.

Jesus said that these things would happen before He returned. *"If the world hates you, you know that it hated Me before it hated you. If you were of the world, the world would love its own. He who hates Me hates My Father also* (John 15:18-19, 23).

Christ also told us how to deal with persecution when He said, *"Bless those who curse you, do good to those who hate you, and pray for those who spitefully use you and persecute you"* (Matthew 5:44).

The apostle Paul said this too: *Bless those who persecute you; bless and do not curse* (Romans 12:14). This may sound impossible to do, but many Christians have done so under intense persecution in the past and even to the present day.

If we are to become like Jesus, we cannot limit ourselves to only the pleasant qualities of Christ. We must acquire His strong traits like standing for Truth, or suffering for His sake, just as He suffered for ours.

We are children of God, and if children, then heirs— heirs of God and joint heirs with Christ, if indeed we suffer with Him, that we may also be glorified together (Romans 8:17).

It will be worth it all someday, because the Bible promises that, *Eye has not seen, nor ear heard, Nor have entered into the heart of man The things which God has prepared for those who love Him* (1 Corinthians 2:9).

Chapter fourteen concludes with a snapshot of the **two harvests**. One is the gathering of the righteous. The other is the reaping of the unrighteous.

*I looked, and behold, **a white cloud, and on the cloud sat One like the Son of Man**, having on His head a golden crown, and in His hand a sharp sickle. And another angel came out of the temple, crying with a loud voice to Him who sat on the cloud, "Thrust in Your sickle and reap, for the time has come for You to reap, for the harvest of the earth is ripe." So He who sat on the cloud thrust in His sickle on the earth, and **the earth was reaped*** (Revelation 14:14-16).

Similar scriptures about reaping the earth point to the same end-time event. *Then the sign of the Son of Man will appear in heaven, and then all the tribes of the earth will mourn, and they will see the **Son of Man coming on the clouds** of heaven with power and great glory. And He will send His angels with a great sound of a trumpet, and they* *will **gather together His elect from the four winds, from one end of heaven to the other*** (Matthew 24:30-31).

Immediately after this event another harvest takes place to reap the unrighteous. [An angel] *cried with a loud cry to him who had the sharp sickle, saying, "**Thrust in your sharp sickle** and gather the clusters of the vine of the earth, for her grapes are fully ripe." So the angel thrust his sickle into the earth and gathered the vine of the earth, and threw it into the great winepress of the wrath of God* (Revelation 14:18-19).

This grape harvest of the unrighteous is found in both the Old and New Testaments. The one trampling the grapes is Jesus. *I have trodden the winepress alone, and from the peoples no one was with Me. For I have trodden them in My anger, and trampled them in My fury; Their blood is sprinkled upon My garments, and I have stained all My robes* (Isaiah 63:3).

Put in the sickle, for the harvest is ripe. Come, go down; for the winepress is full, the vats overflow—For their wickedness is great. Multitudes, multitudes in the valley of decision!
*For **the day of the Lord is near in the valley of decision. The sun and moon will grow dark, and the stars will diminish their brightness. The Lord also will roar** from Zion, and utter His voice from Jerusalem; **The heavens and earth will shake;** but the Lord will be a shelter for His people* (Joel 3:13-16).

These are the same events we see in other scriptures that refer to the return of Jesus.

He (Jesus) *was clothed with a robe dipped in blood, and His name is called The Word of God. And the armies in heaven, clothed in fine linen, white and clean, followed Him on white horses. Now out of His mouth goes a sharp sword, that with it He should strike the nations. And He Himself will rule them with a rod of iron.* **He Himself treads the winepress of the fierceness and wrath of Almighty God** (Revelation 19:13-15).

REVELATION 15 AND 16 were covered earlier in the chapter: "The Seven Trumpets and Seven Bowls," which appear to run concurrently, because the judgments are very similar. They may also be a culmination of the same events that intensify over time.

The Drunk Harlot and Her Fate

Revelation 17 provides more details about the false prophet's power, along with added descriptions of what will take place between this false global religious system (the great harlot) and the global Government and its leaders before Christ returns.

"Come, I will show you the judgment of the great harlot who sits on many waters (people)*, with whom the kings of the earth committed fornication, and the inhabitants of the earth were made drunk with the wine of her fornication"* (Revelation 17:1-2).

According to this verse, a great many people on earth have been made "drunk" by this system's unfaithful teachings. (The faithful church is always referred to as the faithful bride of Christ.) The false religious system is aptly named the great prostitute or harlot, because she has strayed from Christ and His purpose in coming to earth. This compromised religious system is more concerned with the ways of the world than showing people the way of salvation through faith in Christ and His redeeming work on the cross.

This "woman" has a powerful influence over the end-time world leaders. We know this because she is sitting on (controlling) the Beast (the global government).

I saw a woman sitting on a scarlet beast which was full of names of blasphemy, having seven heads and ten horns (Revelation 17:3).

This is the same red dragon or Satan empowered beast that we saw in Revelation 13:1. The seven heads represent seven nations (or governments), and the ten horns represent leaders that will all unite for one global purpose.

*The woman was arrayed in purple and scarlet, and adorned with gold and precious stones and pearls, having in her hand a golden cup full of abominations and the filthiness of her fornication. And on her forehead a name was written: MYSTERY, BABYLON THE GREAT, THE **MOTHER** OF HARLOTS AND OF THE ABOMINATIONS OF THE EARTH. I saw **the woman, drunk with the blood of the saints and with the blood of the martyrs of Jesus*** (Revelation 17:3-6).

This "mother" of the unfaithful is sitting on the same beast with ten horns mentioned in Daniel's vision (7:7-8, 20-25). This same ten nation ruling empire is also represented by the ten toes in Nebuchadnezzar's dream (Daniel 2:42-47).

The harlot sitting on this beast symbolizes her dominance and power. We also know that this system is very rich because the woman is wearing purple, scarlet, and expensive jewelry. She is also **drunk with the blood of God's people**, which tells us that this is the false prophet who enforced the Mark of the Beast by killing those who refuse to comply (Revelation 13:15).

This woman also appears drunk to the apostle John. We know that the more intoxicated a person becomes, the more their behavior changes. They will often say and do things they normally wouldn't do or say when sober. Judgment is impaired, words are slurred, violence erupts when they don't get their way.

People who are drunk usually fail the sobriety test of remembering simple tasks and walking a straight line. The same thing is happening here with this global religious system. The harlot church has staggered from the faith, "forgotten" the gospel, and slurred the Word of God, much to the demise of those who follow *her* wayward ways: *The inhabitants of the earth were made drunk with the wine of her fornication* (Revelation 17:2, 5).

*The seven heads of the beast represent **the seven hills where the woman rules. They also represent seven kings**. Five kings have already fallen, the sixth now reigns, and the seventh is yet to come, but his reign will be brief* (Revelation 17: 9-10).

This end-time religious system will have strong ties to Rome (the City of Seven Hills). The angel told the apostle John that the ruler "yet to come" will reign during the tribulation period. The previous leaders ruled during the Roman Empire and that is why when John saw the final government, he said, "The deadly wound was healed" (Revelation 13:3). He recognized this kingdom, because he was alive during its time, but here, John is seeing a similar government again, only this time it's in the future.

Some people believe that the harlot riding the beast could be Washington DC, because it has seven hills. They also believe this because America was originally settled and based on Christian principles, while parts of its government and architecture were modeled after Rome. This is obvious when we compare the Capitol Dome and the Washington

Monument to St. Peter's Basilica and the Vatican Obelisk in Rome.

Others believe this harlot could be New York City, because of its great exporting trade. They also believe this because the United Nations is located there, which could represent Babylon in Genesis with its "high towers" and many languages spoken at the UN building.

Since both New York City and Washington DC are part of the United States, it is considered to be the one true superpower in the world today. Yet, these two cities don't line up with the sequence of leaders or "kings" that John had mentioned in Revelation 17: 9-10.

"The scarlet beast that was (past), *but is no longer, is the eighth king* (future Satan empowered government). *He is like the other seven, and he, too, is headed for destruction. The ten horns of the beast are ten kings who have not yet risen to power. They will be appointed to their kingdoms for one brief moment to reign with the beast. They will all agree to give him their power and authority. Together they will go to war against the Lamb* (Jesus), *but the Lamb will defeat them because he is Lord of all lords and King of all kings. And his called and chosen and faithful ones will be with him"* (Revelation 17:11-14 NLT).

Here we see the stage being set for the final battle when Christ returns.

"The waters which you saw, where the harlot sits, are peoples, multitudes, nations, and tongues. And the ten horns which you saw on the beast, these will hate the harlot, make her desolate and naked, eat her flesh and burn her with fire. For God has put it into their hearts to fulfill His purpose, to be of one mind, and to give their kingdom to the

221

*beast, until the words of God are fulfilled. And **the woman whom you saw is that great city** which reigns over the kings of the earth"* (Revelation 17:15-18).

This scenario seems to indicate a betrayal or some other conflict between the two world powers who originally worked together, because the beast (government) now hates the harlot (false prophet) and destroys her (possibly Rome) by fire. We know that the city is burned up because John not only tells us here, but he gives us details in the next chapter concerning what is burned and who is mourning its destruction.

We also know that the woman riding the beast is a religious institution, because Jesus uses the term woman in reference to his church when he calls her the bride of Christ. This end time religious institution is the unfaithful church that has strayed from the gospel of Jesus Christ. This is why she is called the whore or harlot of Babylon.

Throughout the Bible, Babylon is always used in reference to any godless or corrupt government. During the time of the Roman Empires, Babylon was also used as a codeword for Rome. We know this because Peter referred to Rome as Babylon in one of his Epistles (1 Peter 5:13). He and others did this to avoid persecution in the event their letters were intercepted and read by the Roman government while in transit. The apostle Peter and Paul were both martyred in Rome.

The Wealthy City Burns

Ancient Babylon was located in what is modern day Iraq, but as mentioned before, it was also a codeword for Rome. Therefore, Mystery Babylon is most likely Rome, because John recognized it. He saw something familiar to him, yet there was something different about it, so he called it "mystery" Babylon.

It is interesting to note that in March of 2021 ties were established between Rome and Iraq. The pope made a historic four-day visit to six cities to establish a connection that would promote tolerance, fraternity, and peace that would lead to multi-faith unity. The goal was to find a common thread (Abraham), so that Christians, Muslims (and Jews) can coexist.

During the pope's visit, no mention of Jesus was made during the peace and unification process. This is because the cross and all that it stands for is the dividing line that separates Christianity from all other faiths. Therefore, in order for these two religious systems to come together in peace, Jesus had to be taken out of the equation and Abraham added in as the common denominator of all three groups.

Muslims are descendants of Abraham's child, Ishmael, who was born of a bondwoman, but Isaac was the *promised covenant child* of God through which Abraham and Sarah's son would be born (Genesis 17:19, 21). The human lineage of Jesus can be traced from Isaac, to his son, Jacob (Israel), and then to his grandson Judah, and then onto King David and his descendants, until the time of Christ's birth. Therefore, God's covenant with Abraham separates at Ishmael's birth and follows the line of Isaac.

This move toward unity through compromise is another prophetic step toward the one world religious system. Eventually, the whole world will be involved in this peace plan that will also be tied to the economy. The U.S. Department of State website declares:

> "The Abramic Accords seek to promote interfaith and intercultural dialogue to advance a culture of peace among the three Abrahamic religions and all humanity. We pursue a vision of peace, security, and **prosperity** in the Middle East and **around the world**."

John's prophecy goes on to say that a powerful angel will descend from heaven and shout, *"Babylon the great is fallen, is fallen, and has become a dwelling place of demons, a prison for every foul spirit, and a cage for every unclean and hated bird!"* **For all the nations have drunk of the wine of the wrath of her fornication**, *the kings of the earth have committed fornication with her, and* the merchants of the earth have become rich through the abundance of her luxury" (Revelation 18:2-3).

This great city and its system are destined for destruction, but there is still hope for those who are involved in this unfaithful church, because **not everyone in this religious system has deviated from the gospel**. There are those who understand God's grace and have received Jesus' gift of salvation by faith in what He did for them on the cross. We know this because a voice from heaven tells these faithful believers to come out of this church.

And I heard another voice from heaven saying, *"**Come out of her, my people**, lest you share in her sins, and lest you receive of her plagues. For her sins have reached to heaven, and **God has remembered her iniquities**"* (Revelation 18:4-5).

Leaving this false church will be a challenge for many, because its traditions and rituals are deeply ingrained in their lives. Yet, it is possible to make this transition by reading and studying the Bible, to discover the Truth within its pages. These people would do well to pray and then listen for the still small voice of the Holy Spirit, as He speaks to their hearts and minds. The Spirit and the Word will provide wisdom, guidance and the power to help them overcome.

The Helper, the Holy Spirit, whom the Father will send in My name, He will teach you all things, and bring to your remembrance all things that I said to you (John 14:26).

As a person reads and prays, it helps to ask questions and then listen for the answer. The Bible says that *The anointing which you have received from Him abides in you, and you do not need that anyone teach you; but as the same anointing teaches you concerning all things, and is true, and is not a lie, and just as it has taught you, you will abide in Him.*

And now, little children, abide in Him, that when He appears, we may have confidence and not be ashamed before Him at His coming (1 John 2:27-28).

The New Testament book of John is a good place to start reading, and then study the book of Revelation (with this book as a guide). Eventually, read the Bible from cover to cover to see the thread woven throughout, which is God making a way to save people from sin, so they can be with Him for all eternity. His Word also teaches us how to live in love and harmony with other people while living in this world.

Jesus is the Living Word of God who became flesh and lived among people. It is impossible to say we love Jesus, and then ignore, deny, or discredit His Word, because they are one and the same (John 1:1-2, 14).

This is why Jesus said, *For whoever is ashamed of Me **and My words*** (teachings), *of him the Son of Man will be ashamed when He comes in His own glory, and in His Father's, and of the holy angels* (Luke 9:26).

It is important to read Revelation so we know what is ahead, especially since this false church does not teach eschatology (end time events), although there may be exceptions. When people have the facts, they are better equipped to make wise decisions and align their lives more closely to the Word and will of God.

The following are just a few examples of how false teachings can be passed down through the ages and eventually believed as biblical truth.

One erroneous teaching is that Jesus' mother was sinless, yet Mary herself said that she needed a Savior.

*And Mary said: "My soul magnifies the Lord, and **my spirit has rejoiced in God my Savior**. For He has regarded the lowly state of His maidservant; For behold, henceforth all generations will call me blessed"* (Luke 1:46-48).

The second false teaching is the perpetual virginity of Mary, yet the scriptures clearly say that Jesus had four brothers and at least two sisters. When the crowds were astonished at Jesus' teachings and miracles, they said, *"Is this not the carpenter, **the Son of Mary**, and **brother** of James, Joses, Judas, and Simon? And are not His **sisters** here with us?"* (Mark 6:3).

These cannot be children from a previous marriage that Joseph may have had, because Joseph was a young man when he married Mary. (Some people believe he was an older man who was widowed with children, but there is no proof of this, nor any mention of other children when the young family fled to Egypt with Jesus, or when they later returned to Nazareth.)

However, the strongest evidence refuting Mary's perpetual virginity is when the Bible says, *He* (Joseph) *did not have sexual relations with her **until her son was born**. And Joseph named him Jesus* (Matthew 1:25 NLT).

The third falsehood is that Mary or some long-deceased person that the church has deemed a saint, can speak to God on our behalf, yet the Bible clearly states that Jesus is **the only mediator to God**. This is because God cannot look upon sin, but since Jesus is perfect, He is the only One worthy to stand in the presence of God as our intercessor. The Bible says, *For there is one God and one Mediator between God and men, the Man Christ Jesus* (1 Timothy 2:5).

Another false teaching is the need for a priest to intercede when confessing sin. This church believes that authority is given "to a duly ordained priest...who has the 'power of the keys,' or the power to forgive sins" (Catholic.com).

Having a priest pronounce absolution, impose satisfaction, and then assign penance is not found anywhere in the New Testament. Jesus is our high priest and mediator. He is the One we confess our sins to, where we then receive immediate forgiveness.

- *Therefore [Jesus] is also able to save to the uttermost those who come to God through Him, since **He always lives to make intercession for them*** (Hebrews 7:24).

- *[Jesus is the] merciful and faithful High Priest in things pertaining to God, to make propitiation for the sins of the people* (Hebrews 2:17).

- *If we confess our sins, [Jesus] is faithful and just to forgive us our sins and to cleanse us from all unrighteousness* (1 John 1:9).

These are just a few of the deviations from the Bible that this system has used to keep people dependent on them, rather than on Jesus Christ Himself. Other topics that are too lengthy to discuss here are Mary as co-mediator (the mediatrix), papal infallibility, and purgatory.

The Word of God provides light to reveal Jesus who saves and regenerates souls. *Having been born again, not of corruptible seed but incorruptible, through the word of God which lives and abides forever* (1 Peter 1:23).

Jesus said, *"If you abide in My word, you are My disciples indeed. And you shall know the truth, and the truth shall make you free"* (John 8:31-32).

Many people will be saved in the final hour before Christ returns, because of what is happening. Natural disasters occur all the time, but these calamities are so unique and terrifying that people will instinctively know that they are part of God's judgment.

In the same hour there was a great earthquake, and a tenth of the city fell. In the earthquake seven thousand people were killed, and **the rest were afraid and gave glory to the God** *of heaven* (Revelation 11:13).

Peter quoted a prophecy from the book of Joel, which also indicates that there will be last minute conversions to Christianity.

The sun shall be turned into darkness, and the moon into blood, before **the coming of the great and awesome day of the Lord.** *And it shall come to pass that* **whoever calls on the name of the Lord shall be saved** (Acts 2:20-21).

These verses tell us that there will always be faithful believers living amid those who do not believe the gospel. This is why Jesus and Paul both command Christians to separate themselves from the ungodly. This does not necessarily mean a change of location (since this would not be possible), but rather a consecration of one's heart *from* unbelievers and the unfaithful, *to* the cross of Christ.

Therefore her plagues will come in one day—death and mourning and famine. And she will be utterly burned with fire, for strong is the Lord God who judges her (Revelation 18:8).

Babylon's destruction will be swift and the world will mourn her fall.

The kings of the earth who committed fornication and lived luxuriously with her will weep and lament for her, when they see the smoke of her burning, standing at a distance for fear of her torment, saying, "Alas, alas, that great city Babylon, that mighty city! For **in one hour** *your judgment has come. And the merchants of the earth will weep and mourn over her, for no one buys their merchandise anymore"* (v. 9-11).

The list of riches is long: precious metals and gems, fine clothes and decor, perfume, spices, oil and wine. John also saw livestock and chariots (vehicles), and the bodies and souls of people who were sold, which may be referring to slave labor or human trafficking.

The buyers and sellers of these costly goods and slaves and souls, will watch her burning in fear of her torment, and weep and wail, because of the sudden destruction of this great city of trade (Revelation 18:12-15).

Alas, alas, that great city that was clothed in fine linen, purple, and scarlet, and adorned with gold and precious stones and pearls! For **in one hour such great riches came to nothing** (Revelation 18:16-17).

Many Bible scholars believe that, because of the description of this "city" and the colors of the clothes and the gold and the riches it possesses, that this is the Universal church and its religious administration. Within this hierarchy, the leaders wear robes of purple and scarlet. The city itself is rich in gold and priceless artifacts.

Every shipmaster, all who travel by ship, sailors, and as many as trade on the sea, stood at a distance and cried *out when they saw the smoke of her burning, saying, "What is like this great city?" They threw dust on their heads and cried out, weeping and wailing, and saying, "Alas, alas, that great city, in which all who had ships on the sea became rich by her wealth! For **in one hour she is made desolate.***

*"Rejoice over her, O heaven, **and you holy apostles and prophets, for God has avenged you on her!"*** (Revelation 18:18-20). [For] **in her was found the blood of prophets and saints, and of all who were slain on the earth** (v. 24).

This verse gives us strong evidence that Mystery Babylon is Rome, because many of the apostles and prophets died under the Roman government. Peter was crucified and Paul was beheaded in the city of Rome. Eleven of the twelve apostles were eventually martyred throughout the empire. The future revived Roman Empire will also be known for its intolerance of historical Christianity and its ruthless slaughter of those who follow Christ.

The final blow to "Babylon" is about to take place. A mighty angel hurls a giant stone into the sea. *Thus with violence the great city Babylon shall be thrown down, and shall not be found anymore* (Revelation 18:21).

Nothing is left to this false system. Only darkness and silence.

The light of a lamp (Jesus and the faithful Christians) *shall not shine in you anymore, and the voice of bridegroom and bride* (Jesus and His faithful church) *shall not be heard in you anymore.*

*For your merchants were the great men of the earth, for by your **sorcery** all the nations were deceived. And in her was found the blood of prophets and saints, and of all who were slain on the earth"* (Revelation 18:23-24).

Sorcery in this passage is translated as *deception and seduction* through idolatry (Strong's G5331). Idolatry is putting other things in the place where only God and Christ should be.

When the bridegroom (Jesus) and bride (the church) are not heard anymore, all hope for humanity is gone. Judgment Day is at the door.

Jesus Returns and Reaps the Earth

After Jesus rose from the dead and lived on earth for forty days, He took the disciples to Bethany, which is located at the Mount of Olives on the West Bank just outside of Jerusalem. This is where He ascended into heaven and where He will also return.

He led them out as far as Bethany. He was parted from them and carried up into heaven (Luke 24:50-51).

After this time, an angel appeared and said to the disciples, *"This same Jesus, who was taken up from you into heaven, will so come in like manner as you saw Him go into heaven"* (Acts 1:11).

In order to fully grasp the magnitude and truth concerning the return of Christ, we need to examine the Bible, which verifies these events through prophets who lived thousands of years ago, and centuries and miles apart from each other. The prophets Zechariah and Joel both prophesied the location of Jesus' return. *In that day His feet will stand on the Mount of Olives, which faces Jerusalem on the east. And the Mount of Olives shall be split in two* (Zechariah 14:4).

In Joel's prophecy we see that Jesus returns to the same place, preceded by a trumpet blast. *Blow the **trumpet** in*

Zion, and sound an alarm in My holy mountain! (Jerusalem and the surrounding area.) *Let all the inhabitants of the land tremble; For the day of the Lord is coming, For it is at hand* (Joel 2:2).

If we put all of the common words and events together, concerning the rapture, resurrection and return of Christ, we can see that they will occur during the same period of time. They are not two events separated by seven years.

Christians are resurrected when they meet Christ in the air right before He returns. *For as in Adam all die, even so in Christ all shall be made alive. But each one in his own order:* **Christ the firstfruits, afterward those who are Christ's at His coming** (1 Corinthians 15:22-23).

- He returns as the wrathful Lamb
- He returns like a thief
- He returns with fire and violence
- He returns with a shout at the last trumpet blast
- He returns with clouds
- He returns with angels and saints
- He returns with disasters and changes in nature
- He returns as the conquering Lamb
- He returns to separate the wheat from the chaff

Jesus Returns as the Wrathful Lamb

Those who know Christ will be glorified at His coming (1 John 3:2). Those who don't know Christ will be terrified at His coming. Whoever is still alive at this time will grieve with such intense remorse and horror that they will beg the rocks to fall on them (Revelation 6:15-17).

Those who are not prepared will be ashamed and afraid when He returns. No position, rank, or social status is exempt from the wrath that will unfold when He returns.

*And the **kings of the earth, the great men, the rich men, the commanders, the mighty men**, every slave and every free man, hid themselves in the caves and in the rocks of the mountains, and said to the mountains and rocks, "Fall on us and hide us from the face of Him who sits on the throne and from **the wrath of the Lamb**! For the great day of His wrath has come, and who is able to stand?"* (Revelation 6:15-17).

These people may have had no faith in Christ at all, or they may have denied Him in word and deed, so they are ashamed and terrified at his coming. Whichever umbrella they stood beneath, they lived life as they pleased, devoid of consequence for a time, rather than living their lives to please Him who ultimately gave His life for them.

Isaiah tells us that these people are proud, lofty, and haughty: *Enter into the rock, and hide in the dust, from the terror of the Lord and the glory of His majesty. The lofty looks of man shall be humbled, the haughtiness of men shall be bowed down, and the Lord alone shall be exalted **in that day*** (Isaiah 2:10-11).

They shall go into the holes of the rocks, and into the caves of the earth, from the terror of the Lord and the glory of His majesty, when He arises to shake the earth mightily. [They will] *go into the clefts of the rocks, and into the crags of the rugged rocks, from the terror of the Lord and the glory* of His majesty, when He arises to shake the earth mightily (Isaiah 2: 19, 21).

Christ's appearance will be so powerful that people from all walks of life will hide and beg the rocks to fall on them. We see this fear in other scriptures.

- *Wail, for the day of the Lord is at hand! It will come as destruction from the Almighty. Behold, the day of the Lord comes, cruel, with both wrath and fierce anger, to lay the land desolate; And He will destroy its sinners from it. For **the stars of heaven and their constellations will not give their light; The sun will be darkened in its going forth, and the moon will not cause its light to shine.***

  "I will punish the world for its evil, and the wicked for their iniquity; I will halt the arrogance of the proud, and will lay low the haughtiness of the terrible (Isaiah 13:6, 9-11).

- *Behold, He is coming with clouds, and every eye will see Him, even they who pierced Him. And **all the tribes of the earth will mourn because of Him*** (Revelation 1:7).

- *And then shall appear the sign of the Son of man in heaven: and then shall **all the tribes of the earth mourn**, and they shall see the Son of man coming in the clouds of heaven with power and great glory* (Matthew 24:30).

People will mourn Christ's coming, because they are not ready to meet Him. The loving and gentle Jesus they had heard so much about is also the King and Lion of Judah, whom they did not choose to believe and obey.

Jesus gave his disciples an example of what it will be like when He returns, to emphasize the judgment that rebels will experience, because they refused to honor Him and do his will. In this passage, Jesus represents the nobleman who leaves (His ascension) and then returns as king (His second coming).

*"A certain nobleman went into a far country to receive for himself a kingdom and to return. So he called ten of his **servants**, delivered to them ten minas* (a type of currency), *and said to them, 'Do business till I come'* (use the money to invest in his kingdom by serving, witnessing, showing kindness, giving to the needy, making disciples, and so on).

The faithful servants who did the king's will were praised and rewarded when he returned. *But* [some of] *his citizens hated him, and sent a delegation after him, saying, '**We will not have this man to reign over us.**' And so it was that when he returned, he said, 'But bring here those **enemies** of mine, who did not want me to reign over them, and **slay them before me**'"* (Luke 19:12-15, 27).

The servants who rejected the king's wishes and rebelled against his authority by refusing to do his will, did not fare well in the end. The king calls them enemies and slays them.

Jesus is both Lord and king who paid the price to redeem us. Though we cannot fathom the magnitude of this gift, we should honor Him for who He is and the gift He freely gave us.

Jesus is all-loving, but he is not *only* loving. He is also just and holy and Truth, which together consist of clear boundaries and moral absolutes.

The world's unbalanced view of Christ has created congregations of enlightened, yet unsaved people who believe in a man-made version of a weak and tolerant "role-model." A meek and mild Christ who approves of compromise and makes allowances for sinful lifestyles.

The only allowance Christ makes for sin is through His sacrificial death on the cross. When we humble ourselves and admit we are sinners in need of a Savior, we have taken the first steps to redemption. Then, when we repent and receive His gift of forgiveness, He gives us eternal life.

Jesus died for our sins, so we would not have to live in bondage to them. *Shall we continue in sin that grace may abound? Certainly not! How shall we who died to sin live any longer in it?* (Romans 6:1-2).

Jesus is God, and therefore He neither changes, nor bows to our will, nor conforms to our sinful wishes. [Jesus] *bore our sins in His own body on the tree* (cross), *that we, having died to sins, might live for righteousness* (1 Peter 2:24).

Many people will dismiss these teachings as a fantasy, but these same people must ask themselves, what if they are true? Is it worth the eternal risk to walk away unchanged? The signs are obvious that we are close to Christ's return. Things that were once inconceivable even a fifty years ago, such as electronic and tracking devices and satellite signals are paving the way for prophecy to be fulfilled.

Violence has increased at an alarming rate and morality has spiraled downhill at a rapid pace the past few decades. Current life and lifestyles are unrecognizable compared to what they were back then. The (figurative) labor pains are getting stronger every day. The contractions are bearing down with greater intensity and shorter intervals between pains as prophecy comes closer to fulfillment.

Jesus Returns Like a Thief

Jesus will come like a thief in the night. A thief is always unexpected, especially if people are sleeping. And like a thief, Jesus will come and go with quick intention to take away things of value (the faithful bride).

- *For you know quite well that **the day of the Lord's return** will come unexpectedly, **like a thief in the night**. But you aren't in the dark about these things, dear brothers and sisters, and **you won't be surprised when the day of the Lord comes like a thief*** (1 Thessalonians 5:2, 4).

This verse is referring to Jesus' return, because it clearly states "*the day of the Lord's return.*" Those who are walking close to Him will not be surprised at this sudden event, because they will be alert and watching for the signs of his return.

- *If therefore thou shalt not watch, I will come on thee as a thief, and thou shalt not know what hour I will come upon thee* (Revelation 3:3).

The "thief" (Jesus) steals believers away right before the battle of Armageddon.

- *"Behold, I am coming as a thief. Blessed is he who watches, and keeps his garments, lest he walk naked and they see his shame." And they gathered them together to the place called in Hebrew, Armageddon* (Revelation 16:15-16).

Then an angel pours the seventh and last bowl into the air and a great voice comes out of the temple from the throne, and says, "**It is finished**" (v. 17).

Since this "thief" warning happens right before the Second Coming of Christ (to battle at Armageddon), the people who are alive when the abomination of desolation takes place will be able to count the days and *estimate* the time of His return. We know this because Jesus gave us a timeline and then commanded us to watch in other scriptures too (Mark 13:34-37).

The precise timeline of when we are to "watch" is also found in Revelation: *The beast was allowed to speak great blasphemies against God. And he was given authority to do whatever he wanted for forty-two months (**1,260 days**). And he spoke terrible words of blasphemy against God, slandering his name and his dwelling—that is, those who dwell in heaven* (Revelation 13:5-6 NLT).

This is the Abomination of Desolation that occurs in

the middle of the seven year Tribulation. We may not know the day or hour of Christ's return, but we can estimate the time by doing the math (Matthew 24:36).

Jesus Returns with Fire and Violence

The day of the Lord will come as a thief in the night; in which the heavens will pass away with a great noise, and the elements will melt with fervent heat: both the earth and the works that are in it will be burned up (2 Peter 3:10).

This "thief in the night" verse is also referring to Christ coming, as mentioned in the section above. This event cannot happen seven years prior, because the heaven's passing away, the elements melting, and the earth burning, would negate all the events prophesied concerning the seven year Tribulation period. This fire and violence is describing His return to battle at Armageddon.

The elements melting with a fervent heat almost sounds like a nuclear blast, but it will be Christ's powerful presence. This violent event is similar to Zechariah's description of the Lord's return when He sets His feet on the Mount of Olives before the Battle of Armageddon (Zechariah 14:1-5).

- *And this shall be the plague with which the Lord will strike all the people who fought against Jerusalem: Their flesh shall dissolve while they stand on their feet, their eyes shall dissolve in their sockets, and their tongues shall dissolve in their mouths* (Zechariah 14:12).

241

The following verses also describe the fiery return of Christ.

- *"For behold, the day is coming, burning like an oven, and all the proud, yes, all who do wickedly will be stubble. And **the day which is coming shall burn them up**," says the Lord of hosts* (Malachi 4:1).

- *Therefore her plagues will come in one day—death and mourning and famine. And she will be utterly **burned with fire**, for strong is the Lord God who judges her* (Revelation 18:8).

- ***When the Lord Jesus is revealed from heaven with His mighty angels, in flaming fire taking vengeance on those who do not know God, and on those who do not obey the gospel of our Lord Jesus Christ.** These shall be punished with everlasting destruction from the presence of the Lord and from the glory of His power, **when He comes, in that Day, to be glorified in His saints** and to be admired among all those who believe, because our testimony among you was believed* (2 Thessalonians 1:7-10).

Watching for the return of Christ is a purifying hope that ensures we will not be ashamed at His coming. The Bible says, *Looking for the blessed hope and glorious appearing of our great God and Savior Jesus Christ, who gave Himself for us, that He might redeem us from every lawless deed and purify for Himself His own special people, zealous for good works* (Titus 2:13-14).

And now, little children, abide in Him, that when He appears, we may have confidence and not be ashamed before Him at His coming (1 John 2:28).

These warnings should keep us alert and encourage us to be living for Christ no matter what the world offers in exchange. When Jesus returns there won't be time to make things right, because in a moment, in the twinkling of an eye everything will change (1 Corinthians 15:52).

Jesus Returns With a Shout at the Last Trumpet

*The Lord Himself will descend from heaven with a **shout**, with the voice of an archangel, and with the **trumpet** of God. And the dead in Christ will rise first. Then we who are alive and remain shall be caught up together with them in the clouds to meet the Lord in the air. And thus we shall always be with the Lord* (1 Thessalonians 4:16-17).

The trumpet sound and a shout were ancient battle cries when an army advanced to fight. This is confirmed in the book of Joshua when the city of Jericho fell. Seven priests carried seven trumpets and blew them for six days. On the seventh day, they blew the trumpets, gave a loud shout, and the walls of Jericho fell (Joshua 6).

These events are similar to the trumpets in Revelation. The men marched for seven days. The Tribulation lasts seven years (or seven days as told in Daniel 9:27). When the priests blew the trumpets and the people shouted on the seventh day, the city fell. When our high priest Jesus descends with a shout and the sound of a trumpet on the last day, all the nations will fall (Hebrews 3:1; Revelation 16:17-19).

The Ark of the Covenant also held the presence of God (Exodus 25:22), and as it was carried from place to place, a shout and the sound of a trumpet preceded His arrival.

David and all the house of Israel brought up the ark of the Lord with shouting and with the sound of the trumpet (2 Samuel 6:15).

We also know that in ancient times the sound of a trumpet preceded the triumphal entry of a king. The trumpet blast let everyone know that "THE KING IS COMING!"

Therefore, as it was in the past, so it will be in the future. When the shout is made and the trumpet sounds, it will not be done in secret. It will be an open show and transition of power as Jesus and his army charge forward to battle at Armageddon.

- *We shall not all sleep* (die)*, but we shall all be changed—In a moment, in the twinkling of an eye, **at the last trumpet**. For the trumpet will sound, and **the dead will be raised incorruptible, and we shall be changed*** (1 Corinthians 15:51-52).

- *Blow the **trumpet** in Zion* (Jerusalem)*, and sound an alarm in my holy mountain. Let all the inhabitants of the land tremble; for **the day of the Lord is coming**, for it is at hand* (Joel 2:1).

- [Jesus] *will send His angels with **a great sound of a trumpet, and they will gather together His elect** from*

the four winds, from one end of heaven to the other
(Matthew 24:31).

- *An angel sounds the seventh trumpet.* (This is the last trumpet to sound in the entire Bible)*: Then **the seventh angel sounded** and there were loud voices in heaven, saying, "**The kingdoms of this world have become the kingdoms of our Lord and of His Christ, and He shall reign forever and ever!**"* (Revelation 11:15).

- *In the days of the **sounding of the seventh angel, when he is about to sound, the mystery of God would be finished**, as He declared to His servants the prophets* (Revelation 10:7).

Jesus Returns With Clouds

The following verses are all referring to the return of Jesus Christ.

*For the Lord Himself will descend from heaven with a shout, with the voice of an archangel, and with **the trumpet of God**. And the dead in Christ will rise first. Then we who are alive and remain shall be **caught up together with them in the clouds to meet the Lord in the air**. And thus we shall always be with the Lord* (1 Thessalonians 4:16-17).

The following scriptures confirm that Jesus returns with the clouds at the end of the Tribulation.

- *I was watching in the night visions, and behold, One like the Son of Man, **coming with the clouds** of* *heaven! He came to the Ancient of Days* (God), *and they brought Him near before Him then **to Him*** (Jesus) ***was given dominion and glory and a kingdom, that all peoples, nations, and languages should serve Him. His dominion is an everlasting dominion, which shall not pass away*** (Daniel 7:13-14).

- Jesus said, ***Immediately after the tribulation*** *of those days the sun will be darkened, and the moon will not give its light; the stars will fall from heaven, and the powers of the heavens will be shaken. And then shall appear the sign of the Son of man in heaven: and then shall all the tribes of the earth mourn, and they shall **see the Son of man coming in the clouds*** *of heaven with power and great glory. And He will send His angels with a great sound of a **trumpet, and they will gather together His elect*** (Strong's G1588 - Christians or chosen ones) *from the four winds, from one end of heaven to the other* (Matthew 24:29-31).

- *Jesus said* [to the high priest], *"**You will see the Son of Man sitting at the right hand of the Power, and coming on the clouds of heaven**"* (Matthew 26:63-64).

- Jesus said, *In those days, **after that tribulation**, the sun will be darkened, and the moon will not give its light; the stars of heaven will fall, and the powers in the heavens will be shaken. Then **they will see the Son of Man coming in the clouds** with great power and glory. And then He will send His angels, and gather together His elect* (Strong's G1588) *from the four* *winds, from the farthest part of earth to the farthest part of heaven* (Mark 13:24-27).

- *Jesus said, "I AM, And you will see the Son of Man seated in the place of power at God's right hand and* **coming on the clouds** *of heaven"* (Mark 14:62).

- *There shall be signs in the sun, and in the moon, and in the stars; and upon the earth distress of nations, with perplexity; the sea and the waves roaring; men's hearts failing them for fear, and for looking after those things which are coming on the earth: for the powers of heaven shall be shaken. Then* **they will see the Son of Man coming in a cloud** *with power and great glory. Now when these things begin to happen,* **look up and lift up your heads, because your redemption draws near"** (Luke 21:25-28).

- *Now when [Jesus] had spoken these things, while they watched,* **He was taken up, and a cloud** *received Him out of their sight. And while they looked steadfastly toward heaven as He went up, behold, two men stood by them in white apparel, who also said, "Men of Galilee, why do you stand gazing up into heaven?* **This same Jesus, who was taken up from you into heaven, will so come in like manner** *as you saw Him go into heaven"* (Acts 1:9-11).

- *Look!* **He comes with the clouds** *of heaven. And* **everyone will see him**—*even those who pierced him. And all the nations of the world will mourn for him* (Revelation 1:7).

247

- *I looked, and behold,* **a white cloud, and on the cloud sat One like the Son of Man,** *having* **on His head a golden crown,** *and in His hand a sharp sickle. And another angel came out of the temple, crying with a loud voice to Him who sat on the cloud, "Thrust in Your sickle and reap, for the time has come for You to reap, for the harvest of the earth is ripe"* (Revelation 14:14-15).

These disasters, calamities, and clouds are confirmed in many scriptures, and they all point to the Second Coming at the end of the Tribulation. Jesus also stressed the importance of watching for signs of His return.

Jesus said, *"Of that* day and hour *no one knows. Take heed,* **watch** *and pray; for you do not know when the time is. It is like a man going to a far country...and commanded the doorkeeper to* **watch.** **Watch** *therefore, for you do not know when the master of the house is coming...lest, coming suddenly, he find you sleeping. What I say to you, I say to all:* **Watch!***"* (excerpts from Mark 13:32-37).

If the rapture occurs before the Tribulation and can happen at any moment (imminent; without warning), there would be no signs to observe. But Jesus said there would be obvious signs to see and show that the time is near. That is why He commanded us to be alert and watch for them.

Titus also wrote that we should be looking for the glorious **appearing** of Jesus Chirst. *We should live soberly, righteously, and godly in the present age,* **looking for the blessed hope and glorious appearing of our great God and Savior Jesus Christ** (Titus 2:12-13).

The blessed hope is the Second Coming of Jesus Christ.

Jesus Returns With Angels and Saints

Jesus returns with His holy angels. Since the angels are the reapers of people, this clarifies the verses that say Jesus returns with angels only, or Christians only. He returns with both.

Christians meet Jesus in the air when the earth is harvested by the angels (at the rapture), and then they return with Him for the Battle of Armageddon, to conquer evil and claim His Kingdom on earth.

- *The field is the world, the good seeds are the sons of the kingdom, but the tares are the sons of the wicked one. The enemy who sowed them is the devil, **the harvest is the end of the age, and the reapers are the angels*** (Matthew 13:38-39).

- **[Jesus] *will send His angels with a great sound of a trumpet, and they will gather together His elect** from the four winds, from one end of heaven to the other* (Matthew 24:31).

- *When the Lord Jesus is revealed from heaven with His mighty **angels**, in flaming fire taking vengeance on those who do not know God, and on those who do not obey the gospel of our Lord Jesus Christ. These shall be punished with everlasting destruction from the presence of the Lord and from the glory of His* power, **when He comes, in that Day** (2 Thessalonians 1:7b-9).

- *I looked, and behold, a white cloud, and on the cloud sat One like the Son of Man, having on His head a golden crown, and in His hand a sharp sickle. And **another angel** came out of the temple, crying with a loud voice to Him who sat on the cloud, "**Thrust in Your sickle and reap**, for the time has come for You to reap, for the harvest of the earth is ripe"* (Revelation 14:14-15).

- **When the Son of Man comes in His glory, and all the holy angels** *with Him, then He will sit on the throne of His glory* (Matthew 25:31).

- *For whoever is ashamed of Me and My words in this adulterous and sinful generation, of him the Son of Man also will be ashamed **when He comes in the glory of His Father with the holy angels*** (Mark 8:38; see also Luke 9:26).

- *For the Son of Man will come in the glory of His Father **with His angels**, and then He will reward each according to his works"* (Matthew 16:27).

Angels and Christians are both present at the Second Coming. Angels reap the earth and gather the saints to meet Jesus in the air, where they are instantly changed from mortal to immortal, from temporal to eternal.

- *The Lord my God will come, and all **his holy ones** (set apart ones - saints) *with him* (Zechariah 14:5b).*

- **When Christ who is our life appears, then you also will appear with Him** *in glory* (Colossians 3:4).

- *For this we say unto you by the word of the Lord, that **we which are alive and remain unto the coming of the Lord** shall not prevent (precede) them which are asleep. For the Lord himself shall descend from heaven with a shout, with the voice of the **archangel**, and with the trump of God: and **the dead in Christ shall rise first:** Then **we which are alive and remain shall be caught up together with them in the clouds, to meet the Lord in the air:** and so shall we ever be with the Lord* (1 Thessalonians 4:15-17).

- **When He comes, in that Day, to be glorified in His saints** *and to be admired among all those who believe* (2 Thessalonians 1:10).

- *So that He may establish your hearts blameless in holiness before our God and Father at the coming of our Lord Jesus Christ with all **His saints*** (1 Thessalonians 3:13).

- *Behold, the Lord comes with **ten thousands of His saints**, to execute judgment on all* (Jude 14-15).

Jesus Returns With Disasters and Changes in Nature

This section brings together the verses that mention similar disasters that will happen when Christ returns and pours out His wrath on an unrepentant, unbelieving world. These accounts are found in the Old Testament, the Olivet Discourse (Matthew 24-25; Mark 13; Luke 21), the sixth seal, the seventh trumpet, and the seventh bowl judgments.

The descriptions below all mention similar changes in nature, such as lightning and thunder, the sun and moon appearing dark or red, a great earthquake, mountains and islands moving out of place (most likely a mega earthquake), terrible hail, and stars falling from the sky.

- *Behold, **the day of the Lord** comes, cruel, with both wrath and fierce anger, to lay the land desolate; And He will destroy its sinners from it. For the **stars of heaven and their constellations will not give their light**; The **sun will be darkened** in its going forth, and **the moon will not cause its light to shine*** (Isaiah 13:9-10).

- Jesus told the disciples what it will be like when He returns: *For as the **lightning** comes from the east and flashes to the west, so also will the coming of the Son of Man be. Immediately **after the tribulation** of those days **the sun will be darkened, and the moon will not give its light; the stars will fall from heaven**, and **the powers of the heavens will be shaken**. Then the sign of the **Son of Man will appear in heaven**, and then all the tribes of the earth will mourn, and they will see the Son of Man coming on the clouds of* *heaven with power and great glory* (Matthew 24:27, 29-30).

- *After that tribulation, the sun will be darkened, and the moon will not give its light; the stars of heaven will fall, and the powers in the heavens will be shaken.* Then they will see the Son of Man coming in the clouds with great power and glory (Mark 13:24-26).

- A similar account is recorded in Luke: *"And there will be signs in the sun, in the moon, and in the stars;* and on the earth distress of nations, with perplexity, the sea and the waves roaring; men's hearts failing them from fear and the expectation of those things which are coming on the earth, for the powers of *the heavens will be shaken.* Then they will see the Son of Man coming in a cloud with power and great glory. Now when these things begin to happen, look up and lift up your heads, because your redemption draws near" (Luke 21:25-28).

- When **the sixth seal** was opened, *There was a great earthquake; and the sun became black* as sackcloth of hair, and the **moon became like blood.** *And the stars of heaven fell to the earth...Every mountain was moved out of its place. For the great day of His wrath has come* (Revelation 6:12-14, 17).

- When the **seventh trumpet** sounds: *There were loud voices in heaven, saying, "The kingdoms of this world have become the kingdoms of our Lord and of*

His Christ, and He shall reign forever and ever!"
*Then the temple of God was opened in heaven, and
the ark of His covenant was seen in His temple. And
there were **lightnings, noises, thunderings, an
earthquake, and great hail*** (Revelation 11:15, 19).

- When the **seventh bowl** was poured out, *There were
noises and **thunderings and lightnings; and there
was a great earthquake**, such a mighty and great
earthquake as had not occurred since men were on
the earth. Now the great city was divided into three
parts, and **the cities of the nations fell**. And great
Babylon was remembered before God, to give her the
cup of the wine of the fierceness of His wrath. Then
**every island fled away, and the mountains were not
found**. And **great hail from heaven fell** upon men,
each hailstone about the weight of a talent* (Revelation
16:18-21).

Jesus Returns as the Conquering Lamb

The word Lamb is used to describe Jesus in the book of
Revelation 24 to 32 times (depending on the Bible version).
This title is only used four times in the entire New Testament
when referring to Christ. It seems that this repetition of the
word *Lamb* is to remind an unrepentant world that it is He,
the sacrificial Lamb of God who was slaughtered, who is
pouring out judgment on those who refused His gift of
forgiveness and eternal life.

The time has arrived for Christ to conquer and sit on
His throne to reign. Jesus returns as KING OF KINGS AND

LORD OF LORDS with his angels and saints for the battle of Armageddon.

I will also gather all nations, and bring them down to the Valley of Jehoshaphat, and I will enter into judgment with them there (Joel 3:2).

This valley is located between the Temple Mount and the Mount of Olives where Jesus ascended into heaven and where the angel said He would return.

- *These* [leaders] *are of one mind and give over their power and authority to the beast; they will make war on the Lamb* (Jesus), *and the Lamb will conquer them, for he is Lord of lords and King of kings, and those* [Christians] *with him are called and chosen and faithful* (Revelation 17:12–14).

Jesus and his followers return to earth in resurrected bodies. Christ conquers evil and begins His reign as King and Lord in His newly established kingdom.

- *Now I saw heaven opened, and behold, a white horse. And He who sat on him was called Faithful and True, and in righteousness He judges and makes war. His eyes were like a flame of fire, and on His head were many crowns. He had a name written that no one knew except Himself. He was clothed with a robe dipped in blood, and His name is called The Word of God.*

  And the armies in heaven (Christians), *clothed in fine linen, white and clean, followed Him on white horses.*

And out of His mouth goes a sharp sword (His Word), *that with it He should strike the nations. And He Himself will rule them with a rod of iron. He Himself treads the winepress of the fierceness and wrath of Almighty God. And He has on His robe and on His thigh a name written: KING OF KINGS AND LORD OF LORDS* (Revelation 19:11-16).

Jesus Returns to Separate the Wheat from the Chaff

The parable of the wheat and tares (weeds) is a picture of what it will be like when Jesus returns and the angels separate the believing from the unbelieving, the faithful from the unfaithful, and the good from the evil (Matthew 13:30, 36-43; Revelation 14:14-19).

- *Let both grow together until the harvest, and at the time of harvest I will say to the reapers, "First gather together the tares and bind them in bundles to burn them, but gather the wheat into my barn"* (Matthew 13:30).

Jesus further explains the parable and tells what it will be like on that day. *The field is the world, and the good seed represents the people of the Kingdom. The weeds are the people who belong to the evil one. The enemy who planted the weeds among the wheat is the devil. **The harvest is the end of the world**, and **the harvesters are the angels**.*

Just as the weeds are sorted out and burned in the fire, so it will be at the end of the world. The Son of Man will send his angels, and they will remove from his Kingdom everything that causes sin and all who do evil. And the angels will throw them into the fiery furnace, where there will be weeping and gnashing of teeth. Then **the righteous will shine like the sun in their Father's Kingdom.** *Anyone with ears to hear should listen and understand!* (Matthew 13:38-43 NLT).

So it will be at the end of the age. The angels will come forth, separate the wicked from among the just, and cast them into the furnace of fire. There will be wailing and gnashing of teeth (Matthew 13:49-50).

It is possible that this is *not* a parable about the division of Christians and the unbelieving world, but rather a division within the Church. Those who may "look like" Christians on the outside, but lack good fruit or the right root as evidence of their faith.

Tares (also called darnel) look identical to wheat in the early stages of growth, but when fully grown there is a noticeable difference in the "fruit" or the head of the grain. The grain of tares are purple and its seeds are black and toxic. Tares are considered weeds or false wheat, which makes this plant not only useless, but also harmful.

The grain of wheat is golden at the time of harvest and contains vitamins and minerals that benefit people and livestock. If wheat and tares were reaped together, the tares would contaminate the entire harvest and the whole lot would then be ruined.

Tares represent those who belong to the evil one and they are identified by the toxic fruit they produce. Wheat represents the children of God who are connected to Christ and rooted in Him, and as a result, good fruit is produced (Galatians 5:22-23).

The Bible says, *May you always be filled with the fruit of your salvation—the righteous character produced in your life by Jesus Christ* (Philippians 1:11 NLT).

If this parable and explanation was not clear enough, Jesus repeated again what will happen to those who lack good fruit. [Jesus] *winnowing fan is in His hand, and **He will thoroughly clean out His threshing floor**, and gather His wheat into the barn; but He will burn up the chaff with unquenchable fire* (Matthew 3:12; Luke 3:17).

Chaff is the outer hull of the grain. The empty shell that is inedible and worthless. Jesus said, *"Every tree that does not bear good fruit is cut down and thrown into the fire"* (Matthew 7:19).

Evidence of fruit (or lack thereof) was a common thread that Jesus wove throughout His ministry. He said, *"I am the vine, you are the branches. **He who abides in Me, and I in him, bears much fruit**; for without Me you can do nothing. If anyone does not abide in Me, he is cast out as a branch and is withered; and **they gather them and throw them into the fire, and they are burned**"* (John 15:5-6).

Jesus confirmed again that this reaping (rapture) will take place when He returns at the end of the tribulation.

Immediately after the tribulation *of those days the sun will be darkened, and the moon will not give its light; the stars will fall from heaven, and the powers of the heavens will be shaken. Then the sign of the Son of Man will appear in heaven, and then all the tribes of the earth will mourn, and **they will see the Son of Man coming on the clouds** of heaven with power and great glory. And **He will send His angels with a great sound of a trumpet, and they will gather***

together His elect from the four winds, from one end of heaven to the other (Matthew 24:29-31).

A few verses later Jesus tells us what it will be like when the rapture happens. *Then two men will be in the field: one will be taken and the other left. Two women will be grinding at the mill: one will be taken and the other left* (Matthew 24:40-41).

Judgment Day!

The Lord Jesus Christ, will judge the living and the dead at His appearing and His kingdom (2 Timothy 4:1).

On Judgment Day in the courts of Heaven, people will be found guilty or innocent based on one thing. The dividing line is what we believed about Jesus Christ and the gift He gave us on the cross.

For without the shedding of blood, there is no forgiveness (Hebrews 9:12, 22).

Those without Christ will stand before Him with no cloak for their sin, and therefore be exposed and condemned when everything is revealed.

The Bible says, *There is no creature hidden from His sight, but all things are naked and open to the eyes of Him to whom we must give account* (Hebrews 4:13).

If Jesus is our advocate and we have received Him as our savior, we will not be condemned, because He already took the punishment *and washed us from our sins in His own blood* (Revelation 1:5).

But just as in a court of law, Jesus will look for proof that this transaction took place with Him. He will look at the fruit of our lips and lives, as verification of conversion and genuine love for Him and others. Those connected to Christ will exhibit outward evidence of an inward change, brought about by the Holy Spirit (Matthew 12:36-37; John 15:1-2).

Since we are not perfect while here on earth (even after we are converted), Jesus' blood covers all of our sins when we confess them and repent of them. We may stumble and fall in our walk with Him, but the desire to live a righteous life will be evident, as we seek to conform to His likeness and do God's will.

When Christ returns as Judge and King, He will look for the fruit of obedience to His commandments to love (Matthew 22:37-40). He will separate those who truly loved, obeyed and followed Him (the sheep) from those who often looked like sheep, but were really self-willed goats.

The two Great Commandments tell us to love God with every fiber of our being, and to love our neighbor (those in closest proximity to us at any given time) as ourselves, even if we don't like or agree with them (Matthew 22:37-39).

These acts of kindness and consideration include those of our own household, who often test our patience the most. Jesus will examine motives and secrets of the heart with a focus on how we treated people, because love is the crux of Christianity.

This is my commandment, that you love one another as I have loved you (John 15:12). This love does not necessarily mean doling out roses and chocolates, but rather giving the gifts of *patience and kindness,* not only to those who are cordial and kind, but also to those who are cranky and unkind (1 Corinthians 13:4).

Jesus took this command a step further by saying, we should also show this patient love and respect to those we deem beneath us, or those we consider undeserving such as those we view as enemies.

"You have heard that it was said, 'You shall love your neighbor and hate your enemy.' But I say to you, love your enemies, bless those who curse you, do good to those who hate you, and pray for those who spitefully use you and persecute you, that you may be sons of your Father in heaven" (Matthew 5:43-45).

When we obey the command to love God and our neighbor, as much as we love ourselves, we are inadvertently obeying the Ten Commandments. This is because love does not lie to a person (or about a person, because it defames their name). Love does not cheat a person (or on a person, because it ruins their trust). Love does not steal from others or kill them, because all of these things cause heartache and pain, which is the opposite of love.

The Bible says, *For all the law is fulfilled in one word, even in this: "You shall love your neighbor as yourself* (Galatians 5:14).

In Matthew 24, Jesus told his disciples what signs to look for *before* His return. In the next sequence of events, He immediately shares three short stories explaining what will happen *when and after* He returns (Matthew 25).

The fate of these three groups is based on their faithfulness or lax attitude toward Christ. They all appear to be Christians on the outside, but the fruit of their lives prove otherwise.

The ten virgins are supposed to be faithfully waiting for Him, the three servants are supposed to be diligently working for Him, and the sheep are supposed to be obediently following Him. Yet in each case, Jesus separates the lax, the lazy and the wayward ones from those who truly follow Him and do His Father's will.

The unfaithful, the slothful, and the willful are all sent to a place *away* from Jesus: The foolish bride is unfaithful and doesn't make the rapture (Matthew 25:10-12). The lazy servant is unprofitable and is cast into outer darkness (vv. 26-30), and the sheep that were really goats, end up in the place of everlasting fire (vv. 41-46).

The story of the ten virgins was covered in a previous chapter, so I need not repeat it here. The lazy servant concerns the one-talent man (or woman) who hid his gift and did not use it to further his master's business, because he was afraid. When the master returns, he does not pity the man because of his fear, but calls him wicked and lazy instead (Matthew 25:18, 25).

The goats were not following Christ because they had no compassion for others, but were more concerned about themselves, going their own way, and doing their own thing.

The real sheep followed the shepherd (Jesus) and heeded His teachings.

Passages like these are proof that we should live in a way that honors God and benefits others. Jesus is *all about salvation by grace*, but He also wants to have a loving relationship with us too. And that is why He made a way for us to live forever with Him.

In return, we should show love and appreciation to Him by doing His will, no matter how difficult it may be. We show our love to Christ by loving other people, by walking in Biblical Truth, by sharing the gospel, by helping people if we can when we see they are in need, and by forgiving those who have hurt us.

When Jesus returns as Judge and King at the end of the Tribulation, He will separate the Christ-righteous from the self-righteous, the ones who were all about Him from the ones who were all about themselves; the selfless from the selfish, and the willing from the willful.

In the following passages we see the final division based on *evidence* of our faith or lack thereof, which is what we did with Jesus Christ and how we treated people.

When the Son of Man comes in His glory, and all the holy angels with Him, *then He will sit on the throne of His glory. All the nations will be gathered before Him, and* ***He will separate them one from another***, *as a shepherd divides his sheep from the goats.*

He will set the sheep on His right hand, but the goats on the left. Then the King will say to those on His right hand, 'Come, you blessed of My Father, inherit the kingdom prepared for you from the foundation of the world: for I was hungry and you gave Me food; I was thirsty and you gave Me drink; I was a stranger and you took Me in; I was naked and you clothed Me; I was sick and you visited Me; I was in prison and you came to Me.'

"Then the righteous will answer Him, saying, 'Lord, when did we see You hungry and feed You, or thirsty and give You drink? When did we see You a stranger and take You in, or naked and clothe You? Or when did we see You sick, or in prison, and come to You?' And the King will answer and say to them, 'Assuredly, I say to you, inasmuch ***as you did it to one of the least of these My brethren, you did it to Me.'***

"Then He will also say to those on the left hand, **'Depart from Me, you cursed, into the everlasting fire prepared for the devil and his angels:** *for I was hungry and you gave Me no food; I was thirsty and you gave Me no drink; I was a stranger and you did not take Me in, naked and you did not clothe Me, sick and in prison and you did not visit Me.'*

"Then they also will answer Him, saying, 'Lord, when did we see You hungry or thirsty or a stranger or naked or sick or in prison, and did not minister to You?' Then He will answer them, saying, 'Assuredly, I say to you, inasmuch as you did not do it to one of the least of these, you did not do it to Me.' And these will go away into everlasting punishment, but the righteous into eternal life" (Matthew 25:31-46).

It is crucial to know that Jesus associates our love for others as proof of our love for Him. It is also interesting to note the type of people Christ uses as examples of who we are to show compassion: The lonely, the sick, the poor, and imprisoned. Those who many overlook, neglect, or see as inferior. Again, how we treat the "least of these" is how we are treating Jesus.

Don't just listen to God's word. You must do what it says. Otherwise, you are only fooling yourselves (James 1:22 NLT).

Are You Ready?

Our eternal destination hinges on the cross. The death penalty for sin is not a popular topic to preach in a feel-good, self-esteem lifting society. We want to believe that we are not that bad, but that depends on who we compare ourselves to. We can always find someone worse than we are, but when comparing ourselves to a perfect person, well that's a different story.

Yet perfection is exactly what God requires if we are to live in His presence. Christ's perfection compared to our sinful natures show us our need for a savior. Therefore, having a sensitivity to sin leads us to repentance, to receive His gift of salvation. A humble heart and a remorse for sin are precursors to receiving this gift.

The Bible says, *The Lord is near to those who have a broken heart, And saves such as have a contrite spirit* (Psalm 38:18). And *God resists the proud, But gives **grace** to the humble* (James 4:6).

The scriptures mention repentance numerous times, as quoted earlier, but it bears clarifying here. To seek God, one must turn from sin and turn to Him. Repentance *is not backing away* from sin or temptation, because in that case, we are still facing the sin, attracted to it, and then eventually yield to it again.

Repentance is not simply *knowing* something is wrong or simply *wanting* to change our ways, because no inward turning of the will or outward directional movement is involved. The desire to overcome may be there, but a person who has not turned their back on the temptation (in thought or deed) is not fully committed to giving it up. They may have a love-hate relationship with a particular sin, which causes them to hesitate or vacillate. This lack of a committed decision is why many people are unsaved (or saved and living defeated lives).

We cannot have heaven and still live like hell. True repentance is when we are *willing* to mentally and physically *turn our backs* on the sin that we love or loathe, and then seek Christ's help to walk away from the source of temptation. The Holy Spirit will then come in and infill and provide the power to overcome it (Acts 2:38). And then throughout our lives, we continue to repent (since we are imperfect) until we win the victory over each particular vice, as we strive to become more like Christ.

This is often difficult to do, because we both love and hate the sin that tempts and entraps us, but when we are *willing to be willing* to let the sin go, the process of freedom begins. Besides turning from the source of temptation, it is helpful to pray, quote memorized scriptures, and then immediately do something productive instead. True repentance is a directional change that leads to freedom, power, and peace.

To those who are unsaved or unsure of their salvation, this matter is the most important decision that they will ever make, because it involves their eternal destination. Not making a choice is making a choice by default.

Salvation is not based on what we do, but by what Christ has already done. It does not depend on whether we gave to the poor, or attended church, or recited pre-written prayers. Salvation is based on what Christ did on the cross and what we do with that information.

We can either remain the same and reject His gift, or repent of sin and receive His gift of forgiveness and eternal life. For those who are unsure of where they stand, the way of salvation is paved in the book of Romans. The Bible says, *For godly sorrow produces repentance leading to salvation* (2 Corinthians 7:10).

- *There is none righteous, no not one* (Romans 3:10). No one. Not a single person is perfect in God's eyes.

- *For all have sinned and come short of the glory of God* (Romans 3:23). We are all doomed by default.

- *God demonstrates His own love toward us, in that while we were still sinners, Christ died for us* (Romans 5:8). God loved us at our worst, and because of this, He made a way to bridge the rift between Him and us. The cross of Christ is the bridge that connects heaven to earth and God to humanity.

- *The wages of sin is death, but the gift of God is eternal life through Jesus Christ our Lord* (Romans 6:23). Jesus paid the penalty for sin by dying in our place, and then gave us the gift of life instead.

- *If you confess with your mouth the Lord Jesus and believe in your heart that God has raised Him from the dead, you will be saved.* For with the heart one believes unto righteousness, and **with the mouth confession is made unto salvation.** For *"whoever calls on the name of the Lord shall be saved"* (Romans 10:9-10, 13).

If we believe that Jesus is Lord, and ask Him to come into our heart and save us (Revelation 3:20), He will forgive our sins and give us eternal life (John 17:3). If we truly believe this in our heart, we will speak it with our mouth. When a person tells another about their conversion experience, it has a way of strengthening their commitment to Christ when they say it out loud.

This can be compared to a marriage ceremony. When a man and woman publicly recite their vows to each other and the witnesses, it helps confirm to them that the exchange took place and solidifies the covenant in their minds.

Salvation is a gift that we neither earn, nor deserve, but one that can be received by faith, because of God's great love and grace. Obedience to righteous living is the natural outflow of gratitude in response to God's inflow of mercy and forgiveness.

Jesus told us to "look" at the gifts He freely offers: *"Behold, I stand at the door and knock. If anyone hears My voice and opens the door, I will come into him"* (Revelation 3:20).

Behold, now is the accepted time; behold, now is the day of salvation (2 Corinthians 6:2).

Behold, I am coming quickly, and My reward is with Me, to give to every one according to his work" (Revelation 22:12).

When a person opens the door to Jesus Christ their life will never be the same, even in the midst of trials, because *The peace of God, which surpasses all understanding, will guard your hearts and minds through Christ Jesus* (Philippians 4:7).

The time is at hand. We need to be ready. *When these things begin to happen, look up and lift up your heads, because your redemption draws near* (Luke 21:28).

Conclusion

I pray that this book has helped you in some way. If you purchased this copy for yourself, I encourage you to share this book with others and secure a hard copy of the Bible, because once these events begin to take place, those who refuse to submit to the Mark of the Beast, may not have access to the Internet.

This book (and others like it that mention the historical Jesus Christ), may also be banned once the Antichrist comes on the scene. There may also be massive power outages when these prophesied disasters take place. Paperback copies of this book and a Bible will be essential references and guides while *Living in the Last Days*.

Please share this message with your family and friends. If you leave a review it may encourage others to read this book and receive God's gift of Salvation through Jesus Christ.

Links to Global Groups and Sources

The Group of 20 (g20.org)

World bank (worldbank.org)

World Economic Forum (weforum.org)

Universal Basic Income (basicincome.org)

Vatican News on humanism (vaticannews.va)

The Economy of Francesco (Francescoeconomy.org)

The Federal Reserve: FedNow
(Fednow.gov/paymentsystems/fednow)

United Nations Sustainable Development Goals
(un.org/sustainabledevelopmentgoals)

International Monetary Fund (IMF.org) headquartered in
Washington, D.C., consisting of 190 countries working to foster
global monetary cooperation, secure financial stability, and
facilitate international trade, among other things.

Document on Human Fraternity
press.vatican.va/content/salastampa/en/bollettino/pubblico/2019/0
2/04/190204f.html

Blue Letter Bible (blueletterbible.org) Strong's Greek Lexicon

COMING SOON!

Preparing for Eternity

Preparing for Eternity will pick up where *Living in the Last Days* left off. It will cover events surrounding the Second Coming, the Bride of Christ, the Millennial Reign, the Judgment Seat of Christ (Rewards and Loss of Rewards), the Great White Throne Judgment, the Lake of Fire, placement in the kingdom, the New Heaven and Earth, and the New Jerusalem.

Books by Carol McCormick

Talk to Me! Listen to Me! Keys to Improve Communication and Questions to Deepen Relationships (Nov. 2014)

I'm Hungry! I'm Bored! Eat and Play Your Way to Better Healthy, a Leaner Physique, and a Happier Life! (Oct. 2014)

The Missing Piece: An inspirational love story (2002, 2012)

Window Pains: Modeling Positive behaviors (2001, 2012)

Your Special Gift: A Preteen Primer to the Facts of Life (1999, 2012)

Printed in Dunstable, United Kingdom